STEAM TWILIGHT

David Percival

Lineside Twentyfive

Left: 'Black Five' No 44727 waits for the road with a freight at Lostock Hall on 4 March 1967.

Below: Tyseley, 1966 – composing the image at the top of page 41.   *Photo by Peter Foster.*

**Published by
Lineside Twentyfive, 7 New Close,
Knebworth, Hertfordshire SG3 6NU**

ISBN 978-0-9566762-3-8

Published 2013

© David Percival

Printed by
Triographics
121 London Road
Knebworth
Hertfordshire
SG3 6EX

All rights reserved. No part of this publication may be reproduced, stored in a retrieval system or transmitted, in any form or by any means, electronic, mechanical, photocopying, recording or otherwise, without the prior permission of the publisher.

With grateful thanks to Colin Gifford and Hugh Madgin for their invaluable assistance in the production of this volume.

Title page: No 60034 *Lord Faringdon* leaves Stirling with the 07.10 Aberdeen-Glasgow 'Bon Accord' on 23 June 1965. Evidently, the front of one of the A4's headlamps has jolted open during the journey.

B1 No 61306 shunts at Stanningley on 29 September 1967. At that date, the 4-6-0 was one of just three B1s remaining in service; all were based at Low Moor and were withdrawn the following day. No 61306 is today one of two preserved examples of the class.

the twilight of steam

THIS book follows on from *Diesel Morning*, which was published in 2012 and similarly concentrates on the period from 1962 until the demise of steam and the end of the 'Sixties. Although I had been taking pictures with a basic camera for some years, it was not until I bought a more sophisticated Kodak 'Sterling II' in early 1962 that I was able to capture the kind of images which I had seen in my mind but had previously been unable to produce.

By then, of course, steam had already been eliminated in some parts of the country; diesel traction had taken over in East Anglia and much of the West Country, for example. At the end of that year, many classes disappeared in a massive cull – notably by the Eastern, Scottish and Southern regions – before I had an opportunity to photograph them. However, a few pre-Grouping types remained at work for a surprisingly long time and I was thankful that I could record some of these veterans on film.

My first railway memories were formed on the Brighton Line, at Norbury, so I had an early introduction to Southern locomotives. On many occasions, on my way home from school, I would stand on the footbridge near the station watching the procession of electric multiple units and the few regular steam workings. I recall that, at about 4.20pm, an ex-LBSCR C2X 0-6-0 trundled past on what I believe was a 'pick up' goods and, some forty minutes later, passenger trains hauled by Maunsell 2-6-0s went by in each direction almost simultaneously.

In 1953, the family move to Stevenage and, soon after, Knebworth brought me into contact with the main line from King's Cross. There, in my formative years, I came to admire all things LNER and I make no secret of the fact that my bias has remained on the eastern side of the country ever since. During 1964/65, however, I shared a flat near Weybridge station during the working week, to be close to my work. There I was able to make a re-acquaintance with the Southern and on many evenings I would be at the lineside with notebook and camera. Steam through Knebworth had already ended and the South Western main line gave me a welcome opportunity to enjoy local steam traction for another couple of years or so – during which time I came to admire the Bulleid Pacifics as they approached their final duties.

Although I owned a car, much of my travelling was by rail. For me, the railway station was an obvious and rich environment in which to make pictures. From the end of 1965 onwards I was fortunate in having a job which took me around much of the country in the final three years of steam. Many of my journeys were to the north-west of England and the work schedule usually allowed me some time in which to indulge my hobby in that last stronghold of steam traction. Occasional weekend expeditions with a friend would take me to places where there was a gap in my coverage of the railway scene. I have to admit, though, that some gaps were never filled; in particular, the Western Region was a major omission which I did not exploit while steam was still active.

At least once a month throughout the 'Sixties, there was a 'shed bash' with the Stevenage Locomotive Society to look forward to. I took part in nearly all of them as they offered so many photographic opportunities. While writing down the locomotive numbers I soaked up the atmosphere of each hallowed location, seeking subjects, angles and lighting conditions which I hoped would make interesting pictures. As a result I was often last to rejoin the group at the end of the visit!

As in *Diesel Morning*, I have grouped the photographs into themes which, with one or two exceptions, follow on one from another. In keeping with the period, I have quoted the times of trains in the appropriate way (am/pm until BR began using the 24-hour clock system) and I have used the then contemporary spellings of names. A journey through the images I have selected for this book thus represents my personal interpretation of the atmosphere which pervaded the twilight of the steam age.

David Percival
Knebworth, Herts
September 2013

Above: One of the last survivors of a long-lived London & North Western Railway design, 7F 0-8-0 No 49407 at Bushbury shed on 31 March 1963.

Left: Nearly all of the 104 J37 0-6-0s, introduced in 1914 by the North British Railway, saw service into the 1960s. Resting beneath a loading gauge during its shunting duties at Dunfermline Lower on 10 May 1966 is No 64623.

Above: A design dating from 1889, the ex-London & South Western Railway O2 0-4-4Ts on the Isle of Wight became BR's oldest passenger locomotives before the last were withdrawn in early 1967. On 5 February 1966, No 35 *Freshwater* approaches Cowes with a train from Ryde.

Below: The last remaining example of three Peckett 0-4-0STs taken over by the Great Western Railway in January 1924 from contractors Powlesland & Mason, No 1151 is at Swansea East Dock shed on 26 August 1962.

Above: For a couple of years in the mid-1960s, the author lived close to Weybridge station during the working week and took the opportunity to photograph Bulleid Pacifics and other types on the line from Waterloo. 'Merchant Navy' No 35025 *Brocklebank Line* passes Weybridge with a morning express from the West of England on 26 August 1964.

Below: One of the last 'Kings' in service, No 6018 *King Henry VI* at Old Oak Common shed on 23 September 1962. The entire class was withdrawn in that year; No 6018 lasted until December but was reprieved to work a farewell railtour in April 1963.

Above right: Removed from a train after suffering an overheating tender axlebox, 'Coronation' No 46230 *Duchess of Buccleuch* awaits its return home to Polmadie at Beattock shed on 15 September 1962. The errant axlebox was the middle one on the left-hand side, identified by the light colour where paint has burned off.

Right: The author's favourite locomotive, 'Top Shed'-based A4 No 60021 *Wild Swan* backs out of King's Cross on 18 April 1963 after arriving with the 12.45pm from Hull. Regular steam working here came to an end two months later.

7

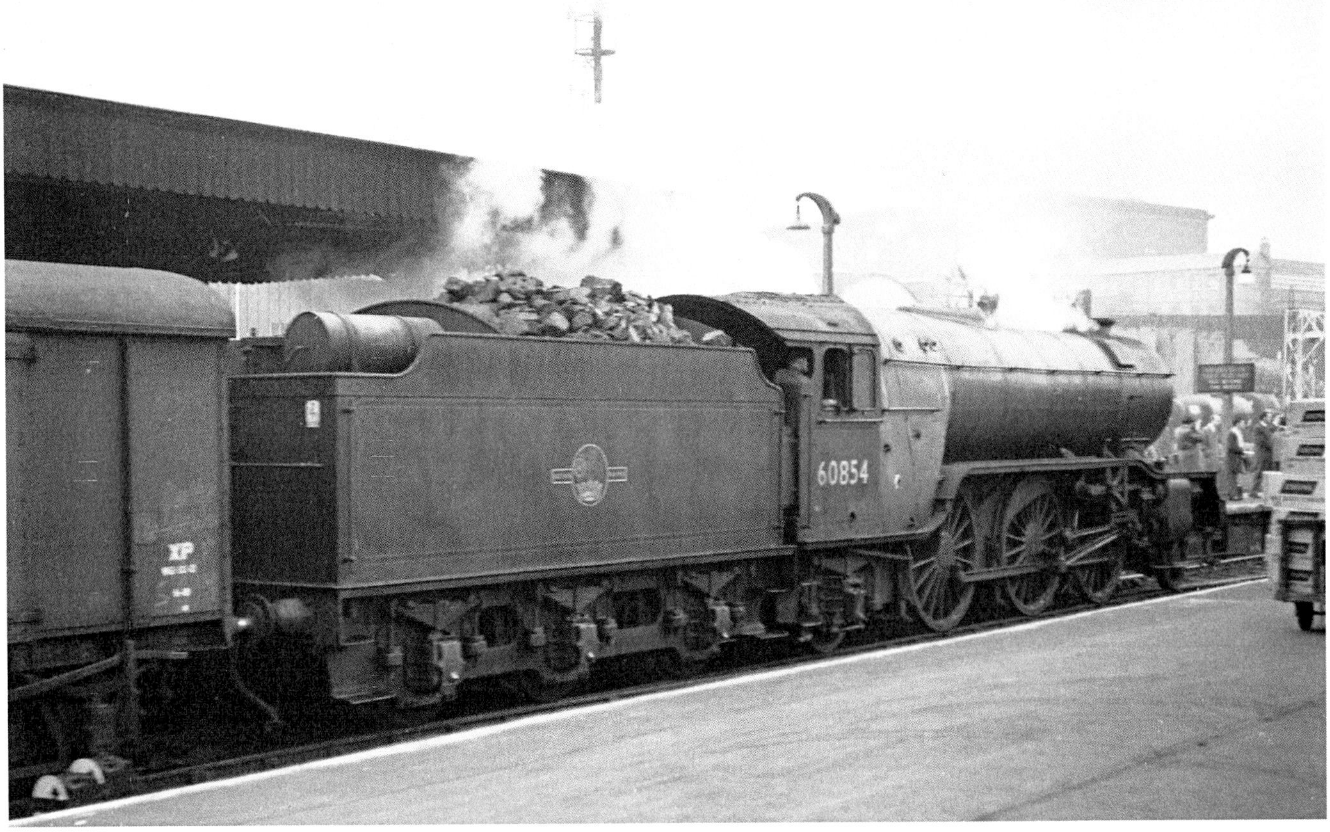
60854

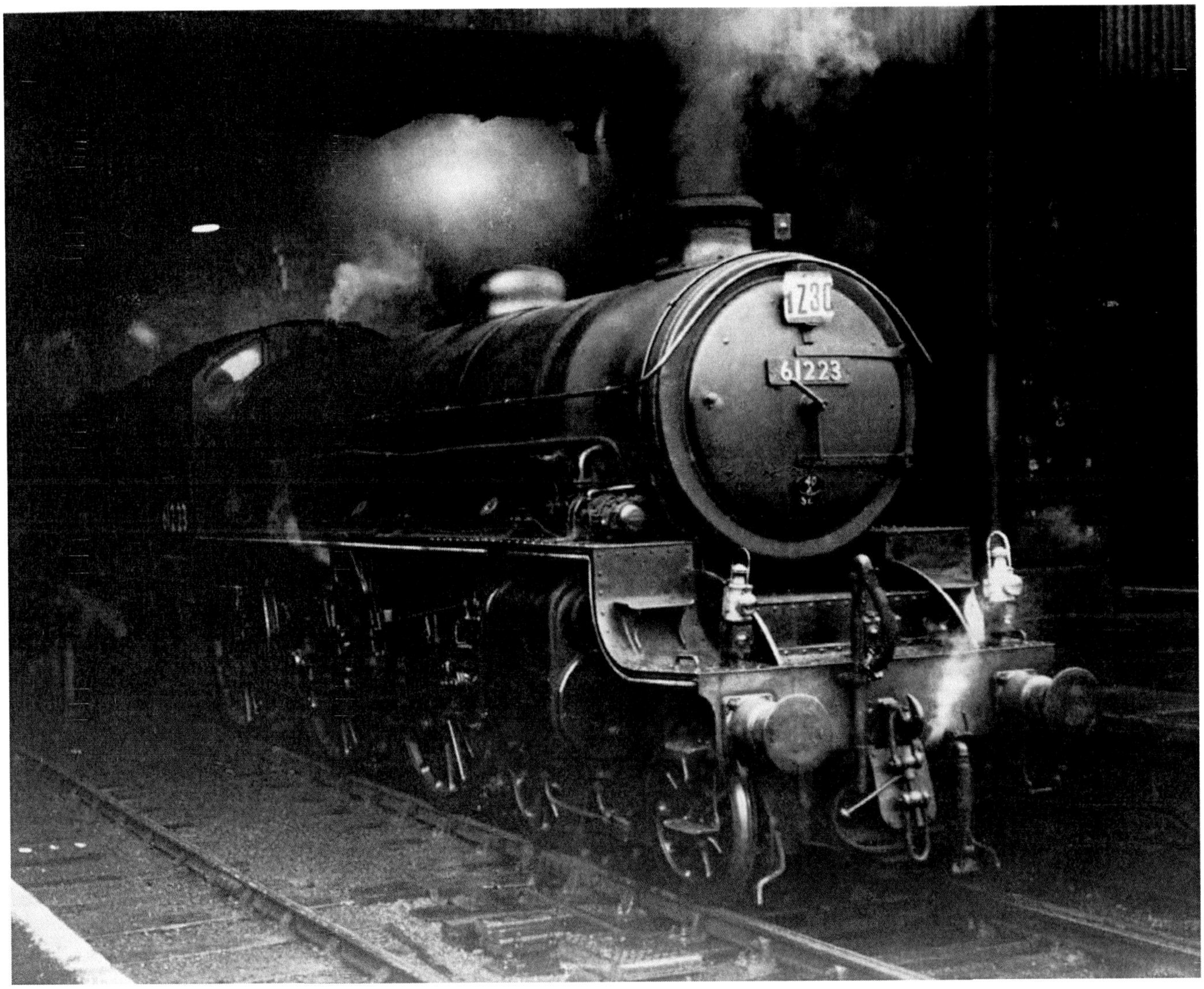
61223

Above: During the last week of regular steam working at King's Cross, A3 No 60061 *Pretty Polly* sets off with the 6.26pm to Doncaster on 12 June 1963.

Above left: The 6.32pm parcels to York was another early evening departure which was steam-hauled to the end. On 4 April 1963 it is powered by V2 2-6-2 No 60854.

Left: On 29 May 1962, Lincoln-based B1 4-6-0 No 61223. awaits its 7.37pm departure from 'The Cross' with a day excursion returning to Saxilby.

Making a typically vigorous Bulleid Pacific departure from Waterloo, rebuilt 'Battle of Britain' No 34077 *603 Squadron* sets off with the 08.35 semi-fast to Bournemouth on 6 November 1965.

Above: Leaving Aberystwyth with the 12.40 to Birmingham on 13 August 1966, BR 4MT 4-6-0 No 75052 passes classmate No 75009.

Below: The Bradford Exchange clock shows Stanier 2-6-4T No 42616 to be ready in good time for its 17.20 departure to Leeds with through coaches for King's Cross, 24 August 1967.

BR Standard 4MT 4-6-0 No 75004 and No 7802 *Bradley Manor* set off from
Aberystwyth on 5 August 1965 with the 18.40 return excursion to Birmingham.

At Peak Forest on 18 February 1967, a 9F runs south light engine as Stanier 8Fs Nos 48495 and 48744 approach with a heavy stone train.

Left: V2 No 60873 *Coldstreamer* stands beside St.Margaret's shed, Edinburgh, on 13 May 1963 as No 60802, modified with separate cylinders and outside steam pipes, runs southwards light engine.

Below: O2 0-4-4Ts Nos 30 *Shorwell* and 32 *Bonchurch* at Ventnor on 26 August 1964. *Shorwell* is about to couple on to the 15.40 to Ryde.

Above: The Sunday morning of 20 August 1967 finds Stanier 8F 2-8-0s Nos 48335 and 48652 at Bolton shed standing quietly with no duties for the day.

Below: On 1 June 1963, A1 No 60126 *Sir Vincent Raven* approaches Stevenage with the 10.45am King's Cross-Edinburgh relief as the driver of No 60139 *Sea Eagle* – unusual power for its Peterborough-London 'pick up' freight – finds that shunting with an A1 is no easy task!

Above: In the yards adjacent to North Blyth shed, J27 0-6-0 No 65819 makes up a train of 21-ton hopper wagons loaded with coal from local collieries on 28 April 1962.

Above right: 'Jinty' 0-6-0T No 47432 moves wagons at Willesden shed on 24 January 1965.

Right: Driver Luckhurst shunts with K 2-6-0 No 32340 at Three Bridges, 23 September 1962.

17

Above: A 9F 2-10-0 climbs towards Heswall Hills with an unbraked iron ore train of getting on for 1,000 tons from Bidston to the Hawarden Bridge steelworks of John Summers on 21 August 1967.

Below: A BR 5MT between Byfleet Junction and Addlestone Junction, on the triangle at Weybridge, with an engineers' train, 5 April 1965.

The fireman of 8F No 48536 prepares to alight and reset the points in the yard of Agecroft shed on 23 October 1965.

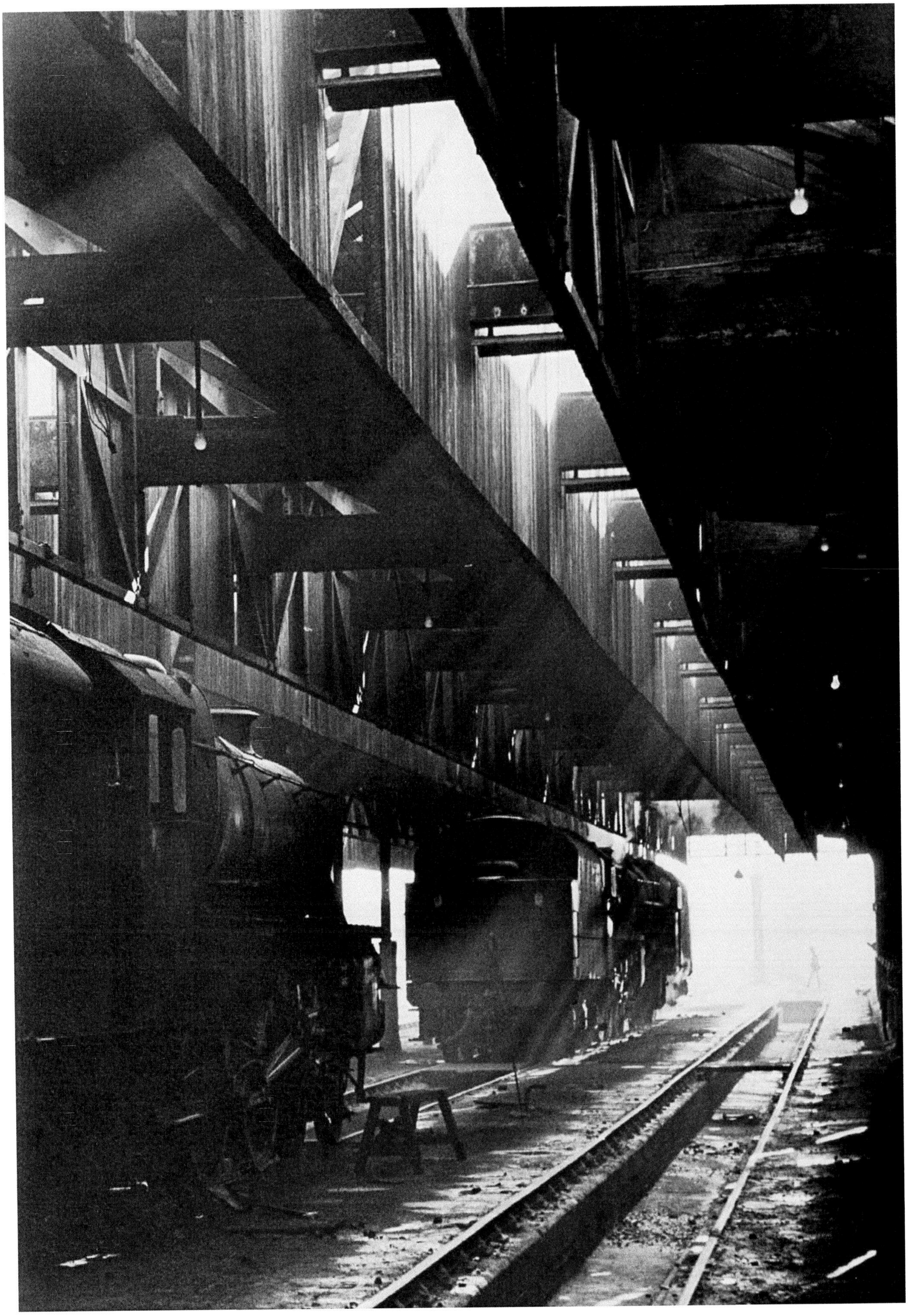

Above: Two and three-cylinder Stanier 4-6-0s – 5MT No 45284 and 'Jubilee' No 45563 *Australia* at Trafford Park shed, 23 October 1965. In the background is BR Standard 3MT 2-6-2T No 82009.

Left: 'Black Fives' and an 8F at Agecroft on the same day. These classes were the mainstay of the shed's allocation at the time.

Below: Also on 23 October 1965 are 'Jubilee' No 45654 *Hood* and 'Britannia' No 70027 *Rising Star* at Newton Heath.

A smoky twilight at Birkenhead on Sunday 20 August 1967, when the
55 steam locomotives on shed included no fewer than 41 9Fs. Many of
the 2-10-0s, together with some 8Fs, have just had their fires lit and are
beginning to raise steam in preparation for the coming week's duties.

The last Leap Year Day of the steam era. As the sun sets on
Stanier 8F No 48257 and BR 4MT 4-6-0 No 75027 at Rose Grove
shed on 29 February 1968, the two footplatemen are perhaps
pondering the future. For the 4-6-0, it would be preservation.

Above: Like its classmate on page 23, BR 4MT 4-6-0 No 75029 still exists – purchased, with 9F 92203, by artist David Shepherd. On 6 April 1968 the two Standards approach Harpenden, on their way from Crewe to Cricklewood and, the next day, Longmoor.

Top right: After working the Bradford portion of the 'Yorkshire Pullman' to Leeds on 29 September 1967, 'Black Five' No 45208 returns tender-first past Stanningley, where a classic Riley RME sports saloon is parked in the engineers' yard.

Centre right: Minus its *Blue Funnel* nameplates, 'Merchant Navy' No 35013 sets off tender-first from Weymouth shed towards the station on 11 June 1967.

Bottom right: One of the Lickey banking engines, 9400 'Pannier' No 8402 propels a brake van through Bromsgrove towards the bankers' stabling point south of the station on 31 March 1963.

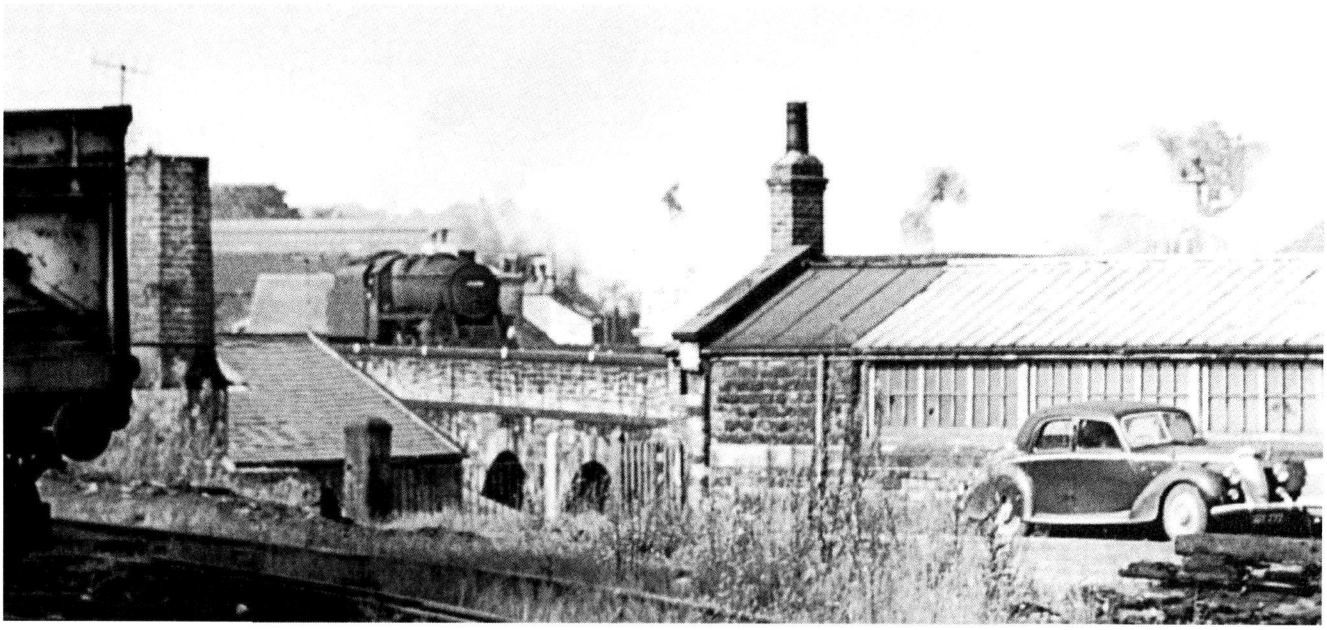

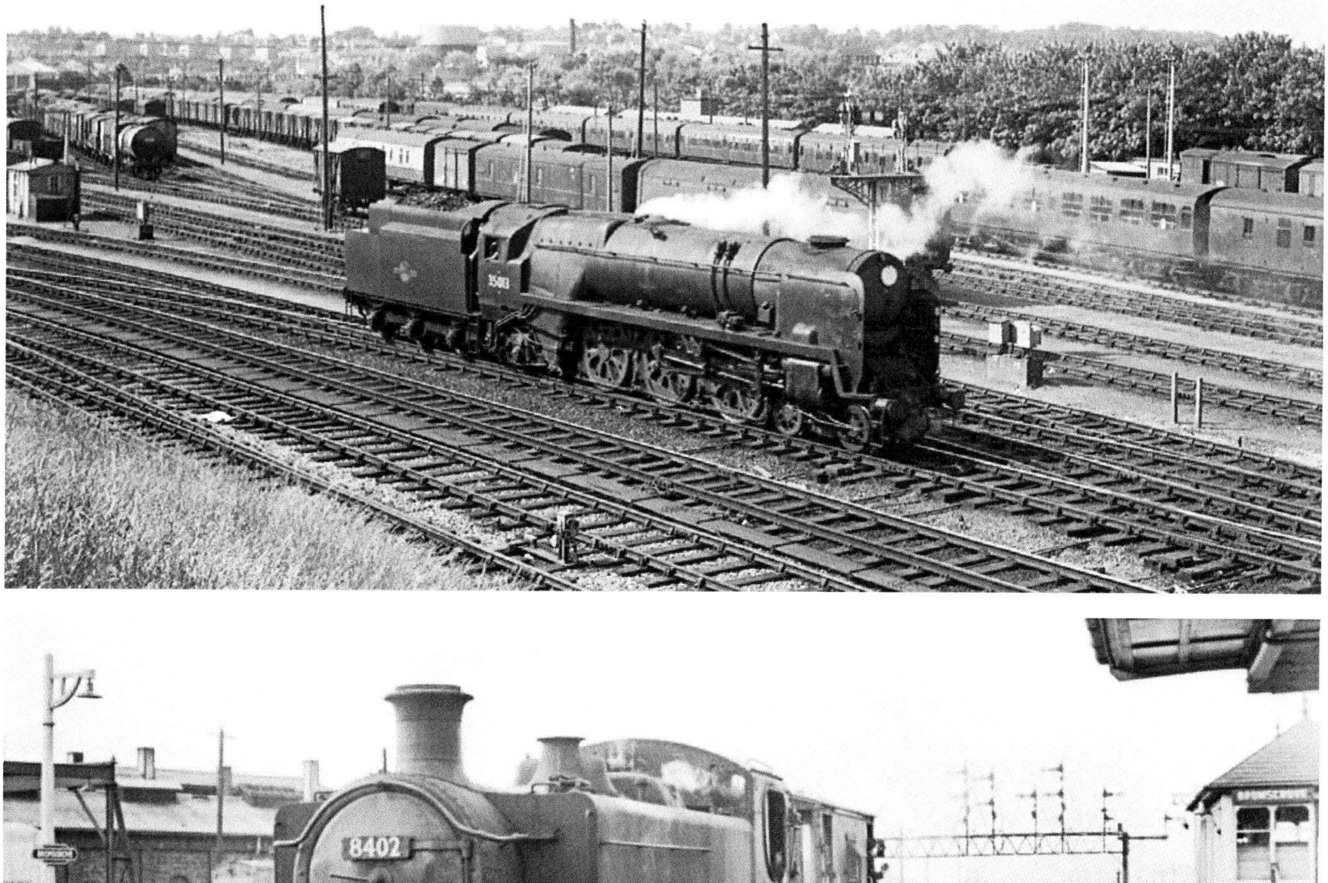

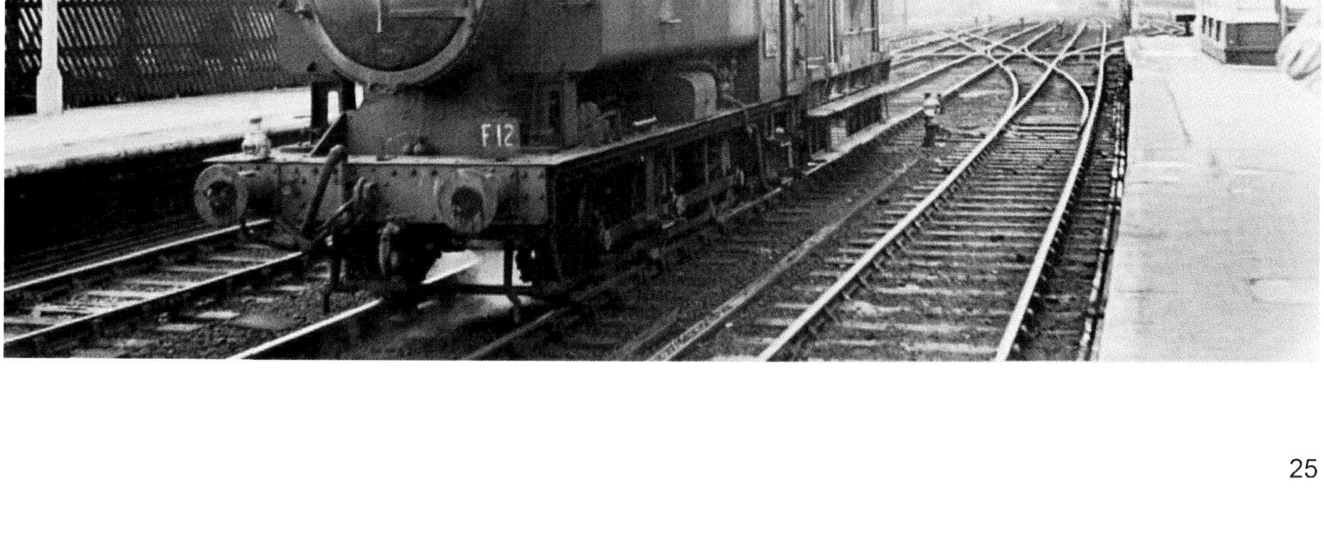
8402
F12

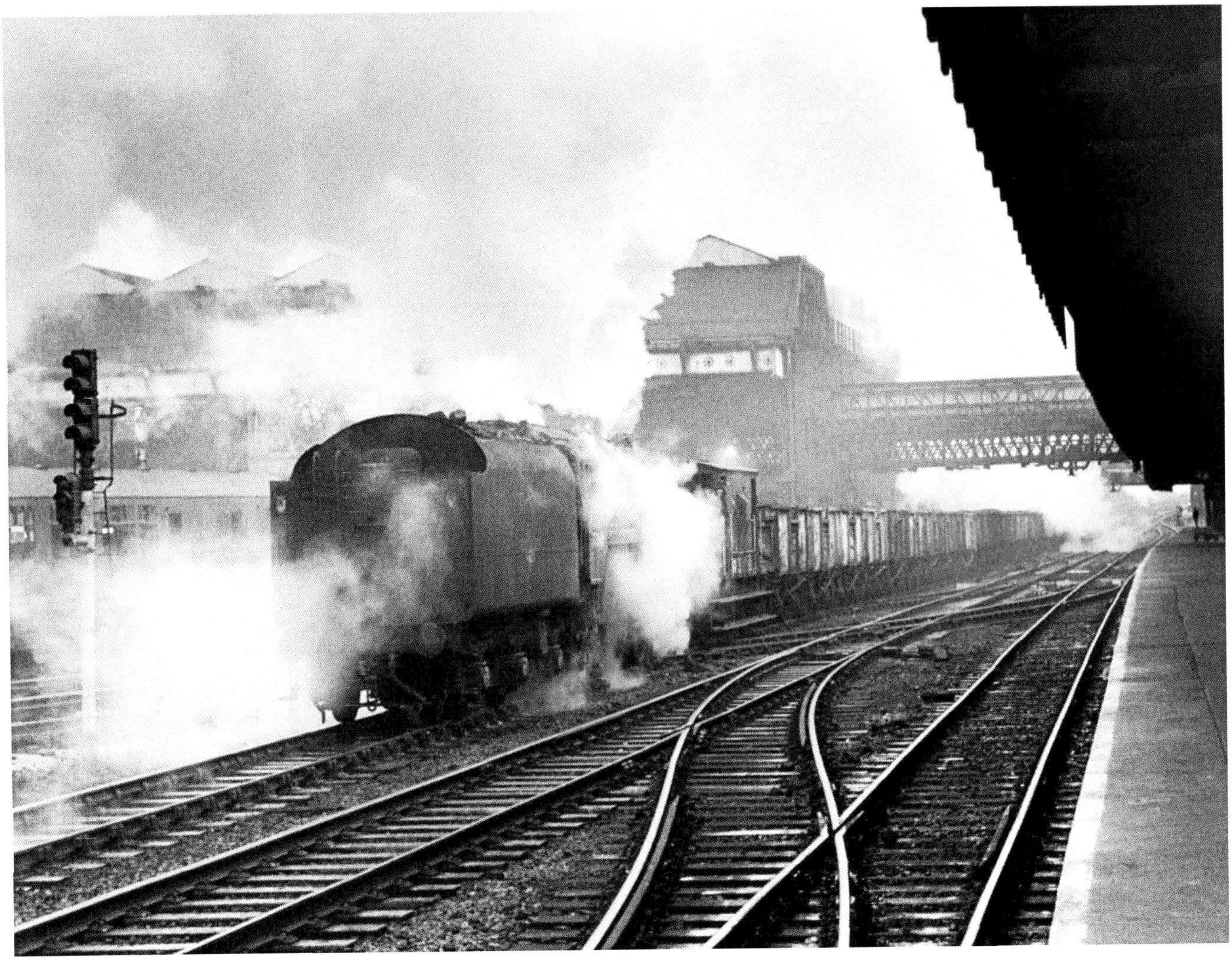

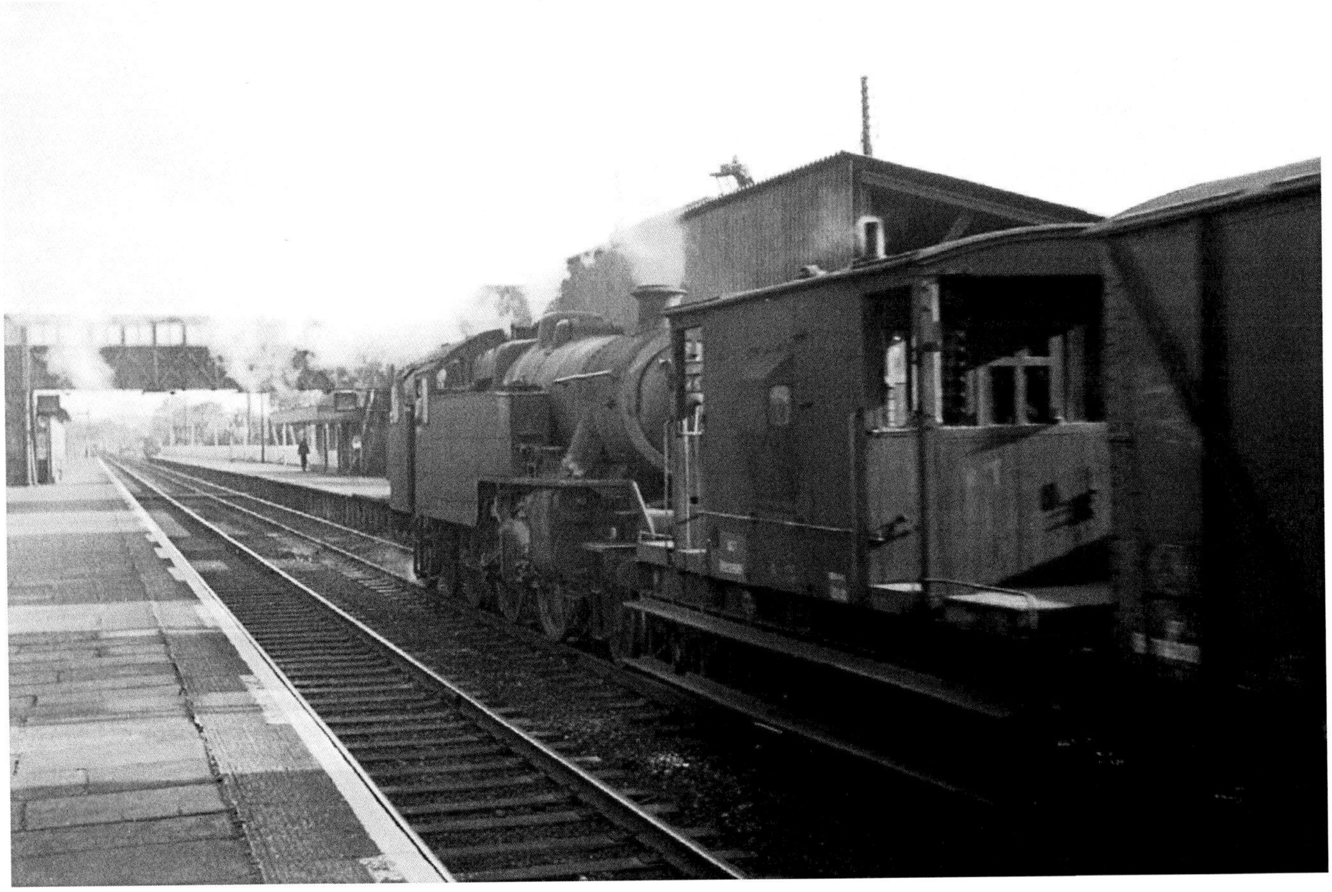

Left: At Manchester Victoria on 1 March 1968, Standard 5MT No 73069 begins to bank a coal train up the 1 in 59/47 gradient to Miles Platting.

Below left: Fairburn 4MT 2-6-4T No 42693 assists a down freight out of Beattock on 15 September 1962.

Right: 'Black Five' No 45297 approaches Shap Summit with an up freight early on the morning of 23 August 1967.

Below: Setting off from Beattock on 15 September 1962 with the freight pictured on the opposite page is 'Black Five' No 45136.

27

Above: 'Black Five' No 45118 passes Carlisle Kingmoor shed with an up freight on 7 May 1966.

Below: Approaching Skew Bridge, south of Preston, on 25 March 1967, an up freight is hauled by No 45455.

Above: No 44804 passes the site of Chiltern Green station, between Harpenden and Luton, with a northbound freight on 11 May 1963.

Right: Hauled by No 44990, a down freight crosses the River Eden as it approaches Kingmoor, 7 May 1966.

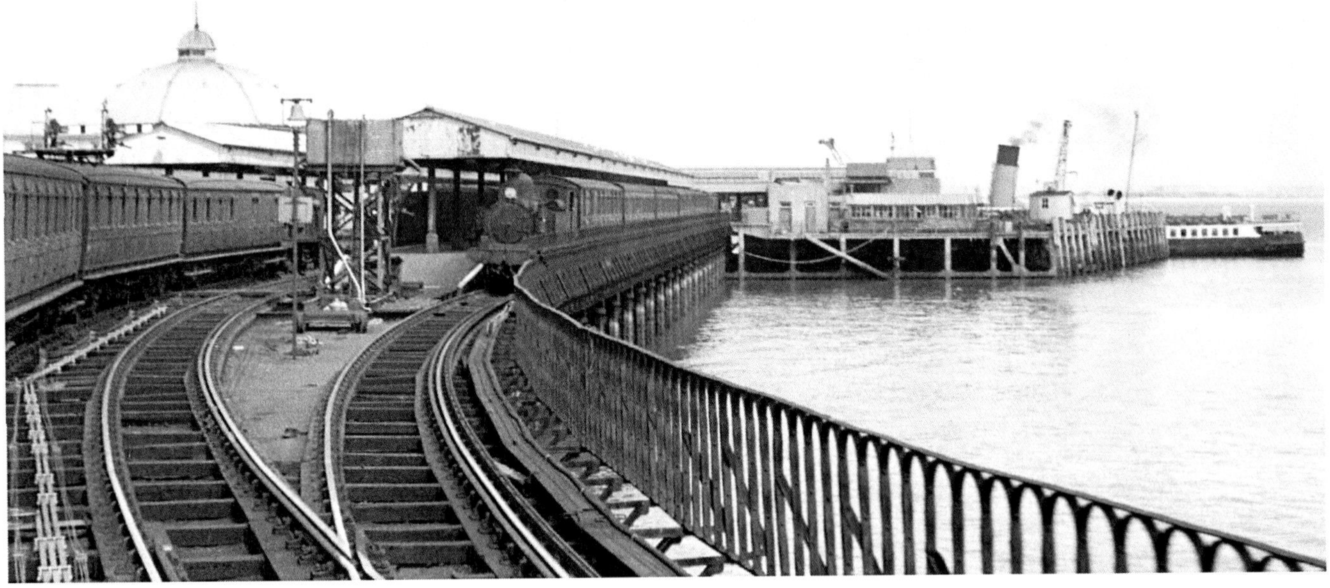

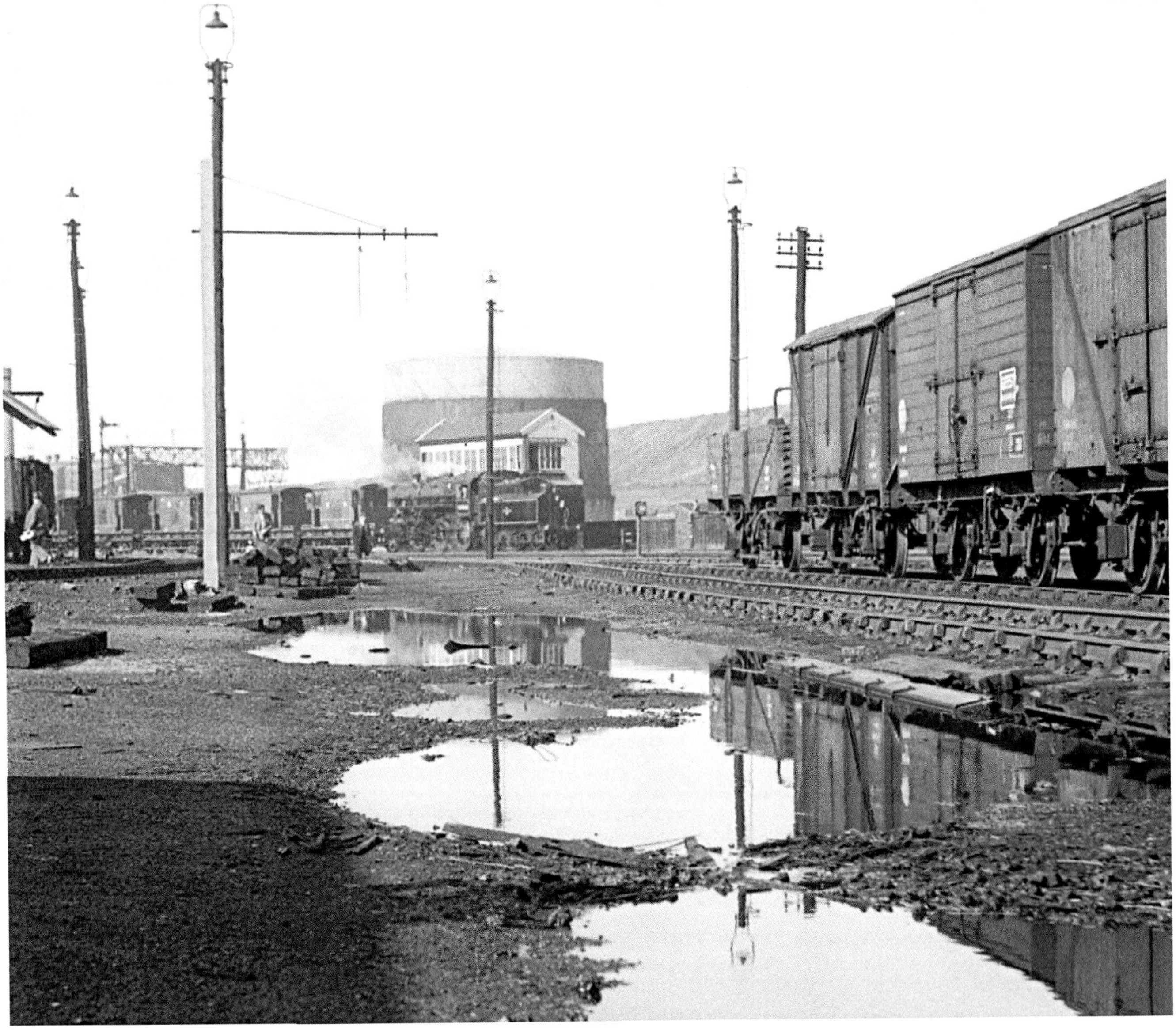

Above left: O2 0-4-4T No 17 *Seaview* stands at Ryde Pierhead with a train for Ventnor on 15 July 1964 as No 28 *Ashey* brings in another load of passengers for the waiting ferry.

Left: Ivatt 4MT 2-6-0 No 43006 prepares to work a Railway Enthusiasts' Club brakevan tour of colliery lines around Workington on 7 May 1966.

Above: A passer-by pauses to watch 'Black Five' No 44683 racing down the 1 in 104 gradient towards Wigan with a southbound express on 19 February 1966.

The fireman drops in the bag for BR Standard 4MT
No 75019 to take on water at Rose Grove on 11 May 1968.

N7 0-6-2T No 69621 takes water while running round the LCGB
'Great Eastern Suburban Rail Tour' at Palace Gates on 7 April 1962.
The open first with the BR crest, at the back of Bounds Green
carriage shed, is part of a former LNER 'Coronation' articulated twin.

Right: The driver has already turned off the flow but water remaining in the column makes a splash after the tender of No 3854 has been filled at Southall shed on 24 January 1965.

Below: Without his fireman checking the water level at Workington shed on 22 August 1967, the driver of No 43006 had to wait for the tank to overflow before taking appropriate action. So did the photographer!

Above: 'Royal Scot' No 46115 *Scots Guardsman* at Kingmoor shed on 21 May 1966. In line behind it are Nos 48280, 45218 and 70037 *Hereward the Wake*; alongside is WD No 90644.

Below: Double-chimney Standard 4MT 4-6-0 No 75077 at Redhill shed on 7 December 1963

Left: 'Large Prairie' 2-6-2T No 6128 stands at the foot of the coal wagon road supplying a typical Great Western coaling stage at Slough shed on 16 December 1962.

Below: The coaling plant and ash pits at Nine Elms shed on 30 January 1965, with four rebuilt Bulleid Pacifics standing in line. Behind 'Merchant Navy' No 35027 *Port Line* are 'Light' Pacifics Nos 34009 *Lyme Regis*, 34056 *Croydon* and 34093 *Saunton*.

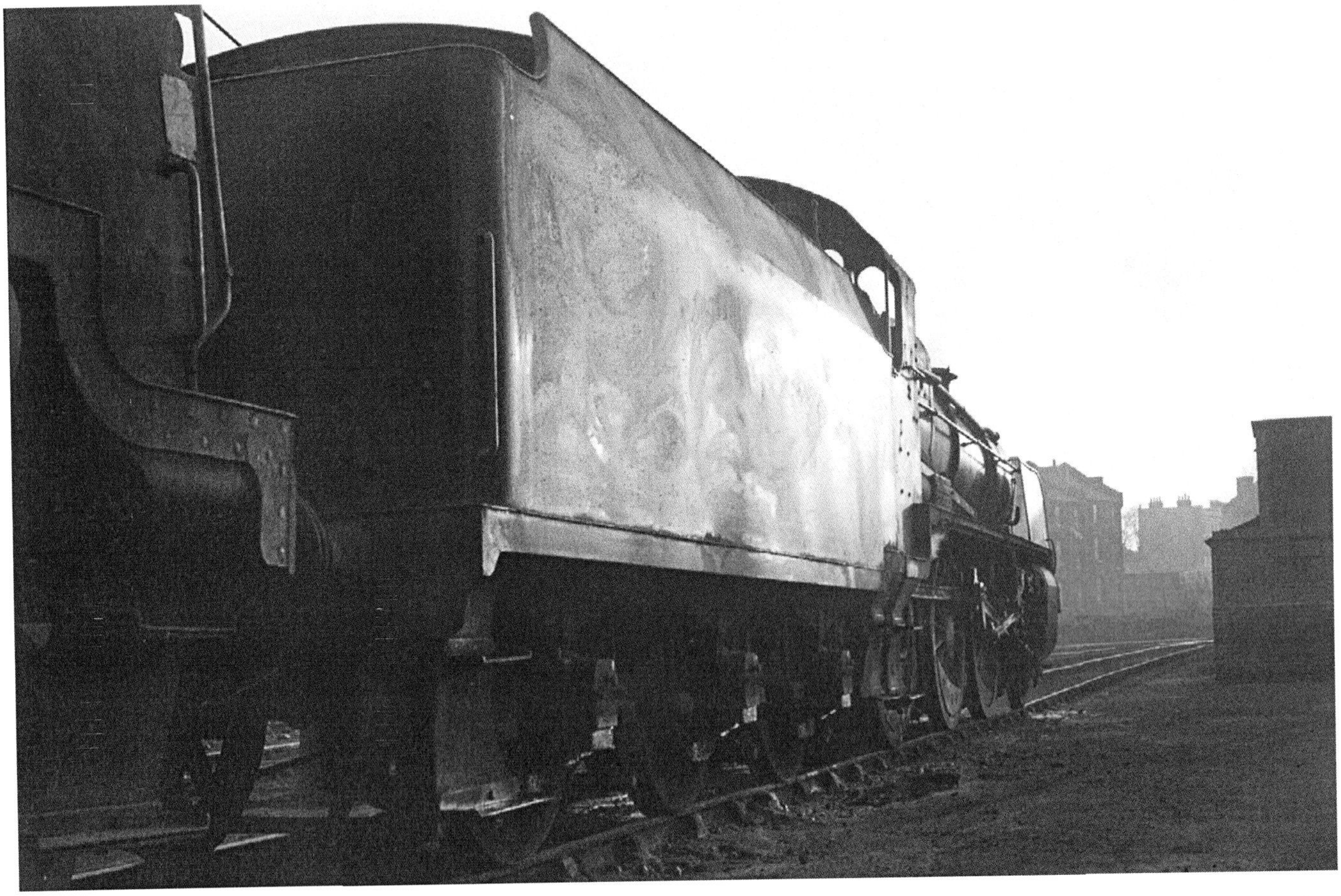

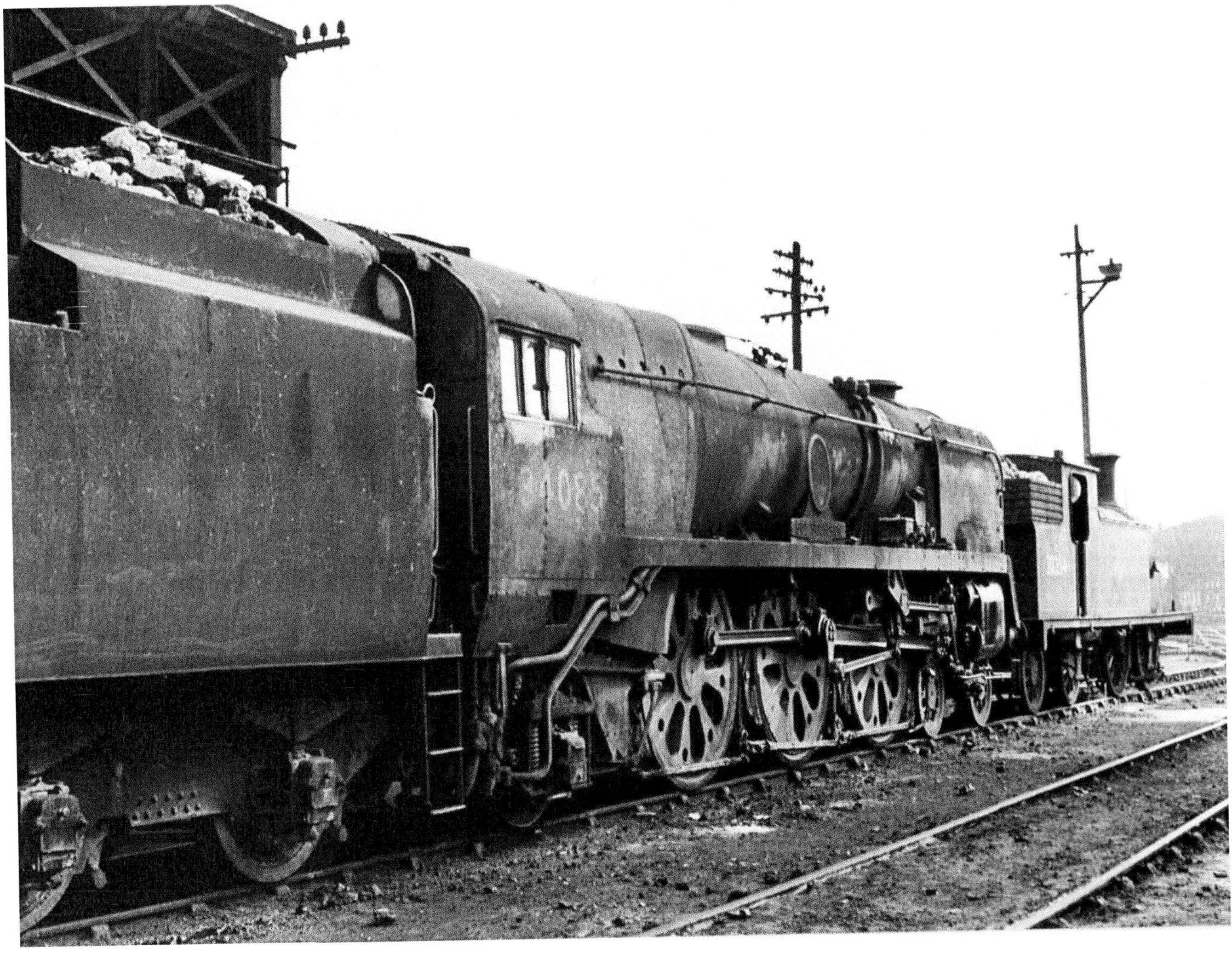

Left: Standing in the yard at Norwood Junction shed on 7 December 1963, N 2-6-0 No 31401 glints in the low winter sunshine.

Below left: A mixture of soot, coal dust, oil and general filth clings to No 34085 *501 Squadron*, on shed at Bournemouth with M7 0-4-4T No 30254 on 22 March 1964. Such a grimy appearance was not unusual in the final years of the Bulleid Pacifics.

Right: Compared with its rebuilt classmate, No 34076 *41 Squadron* is well turned-out at Feltham shed on 24 January 1965.

Below: A similar but rather less dramatic contrast in cleanliness at Redhill on 16 June 1963 – consecutively-numbered S15 4-6-0s Nos 30835 and 30836.

37

Above: Entering service together in 1953, Standard 2MTs Nos 78012 and 78013 were withdrawn together in May 1967. On 20 August 1967 they await removal from Bolton shed.

Below: Stored at Kingmoor on 17 May 1963 are No 46200 *The Princess Royal* in red livery and No 46201 *Princess Elizabeth* in green.

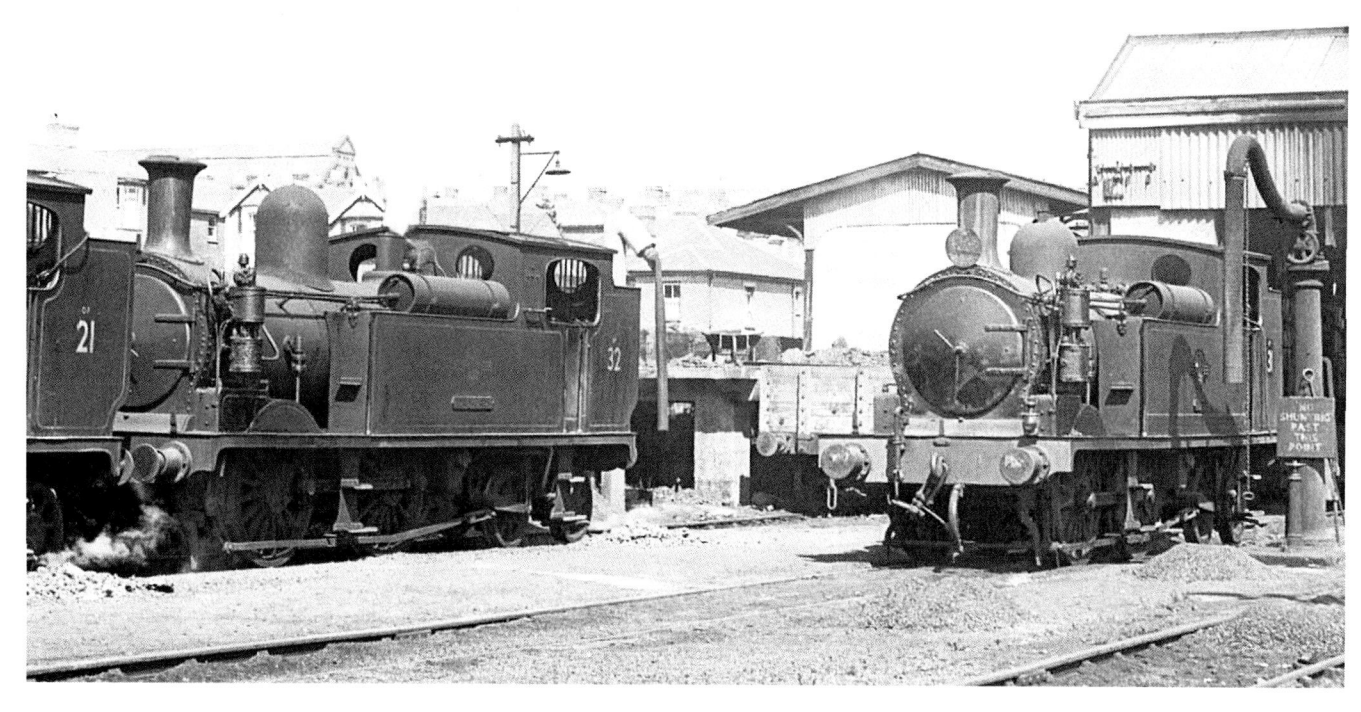

O2 0-4-4Ts Nos 31 *Chale* and 32 *Bonchurch* stand outside the shed at Ryde with classmate No 21 *Sandown* on 26 August 1964.

B1 4-6-0s Nos 61050 and 61051 in the roundhouse at Canklow on 2 October 1965.

Above: J27 0-6-0s Nos 65882, 65811 and 65892 at Sunderland on 20 May 1967. Nos 65811 and 65882 became two of the last five J27s in service, all withdrawn in the week ending 9 September 1967.

Below: Driver Willetts and fireman Edgington turn 9F No 92013 at Saltley on 27 March 1966, flanked by Nos 92218 and 92164. The latter 2-10-0 has acquired a BR1G tender in place of its original BR1C type.

Above: The lack of a smoke hood above No 45134 is evident as the 'Black Five' brews up alongside No 45287 at Tyseley on 27 March 1966.

Right: Shafts of sunlight penetrate the roundhouse at Aberdare as members of the Stevenage Locomotive Society collect the numbers of 5700 0-6-0PTs Nos 4688 and 3716, together with 4200 2-8-0T No 4299, on 8 September 1963.

Right: On 4 March 1967, 9F No 92014 finds itself under the spotlight in the roundhouse at Holbeck.

Opposite, upper: V2 2-6-2 No 60846, A3 No 60041 *Salmon Trout* and B1 No 61099 at St.Margaret's shed, Edinburgh, on 25 June 1965. 'Black Five' No 45235 stands by the coaling stage.

Opposite, lower: No 60010 *Dominion of Canada* and No 60030 *Golden Fleece* at King's Cross shed on 19 January 1963. The latter had been withdrawn at the end of December and, in the harsh weather of that winter, icicles have formed on the streamlined casing.

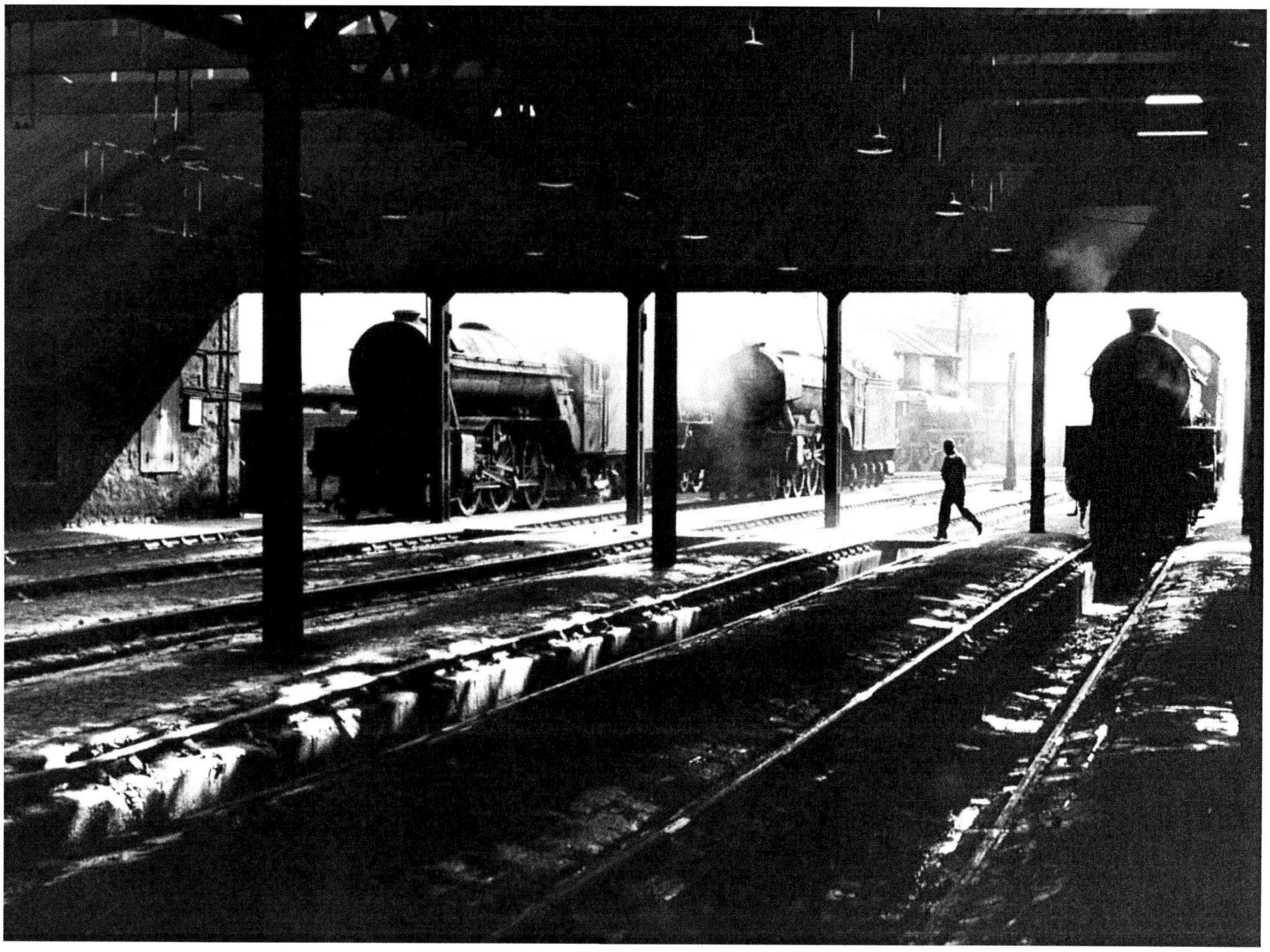

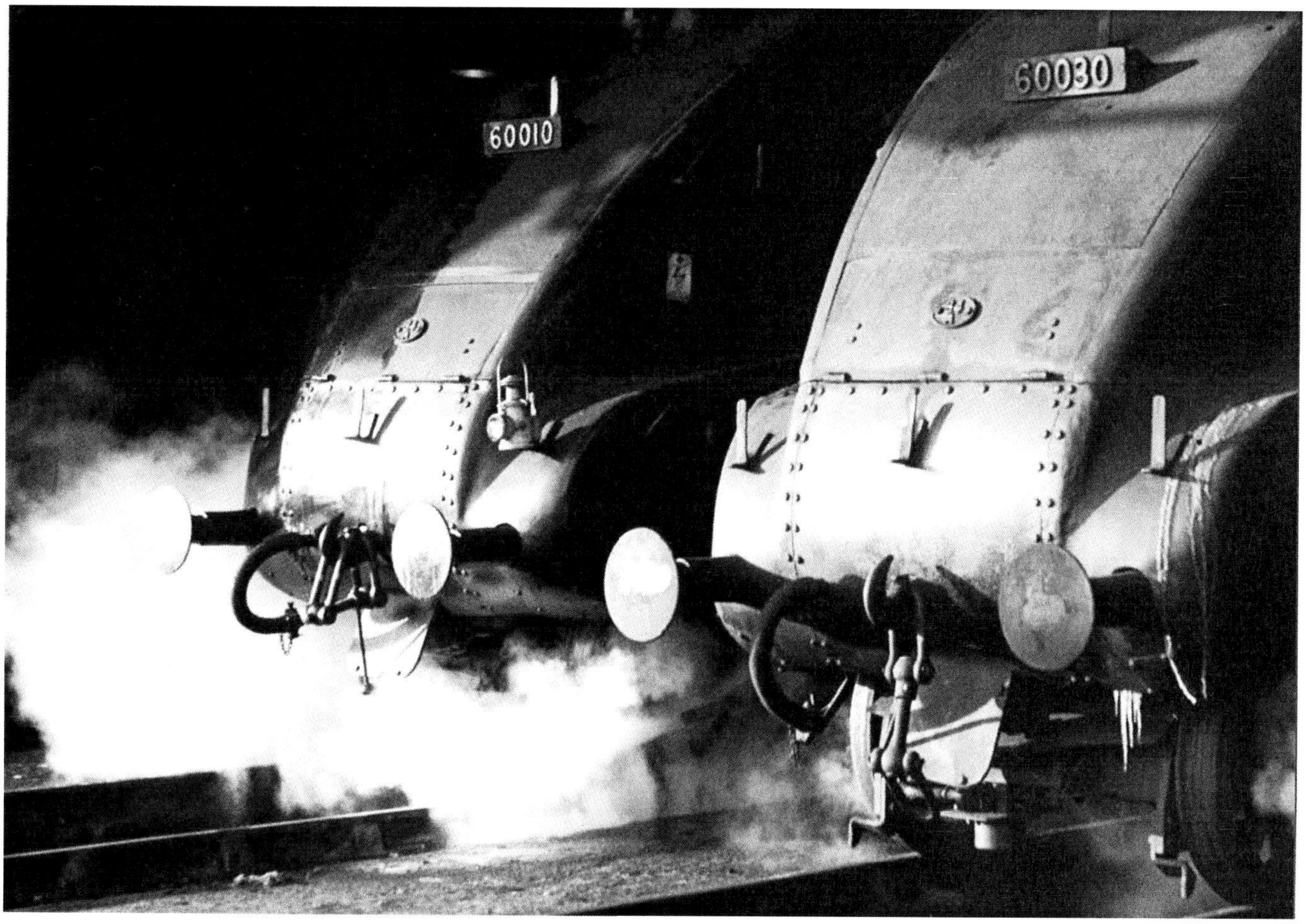
60010
60030

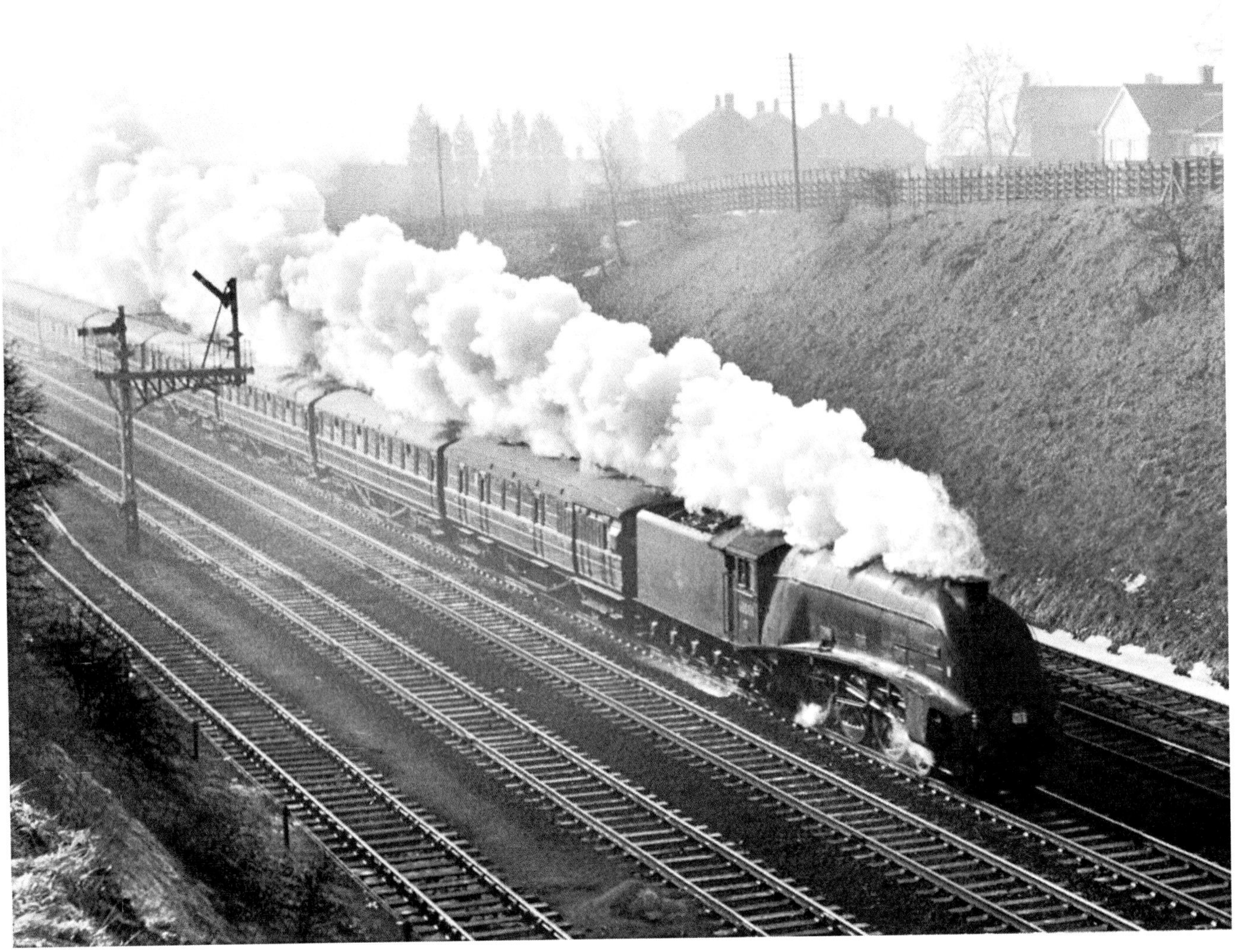

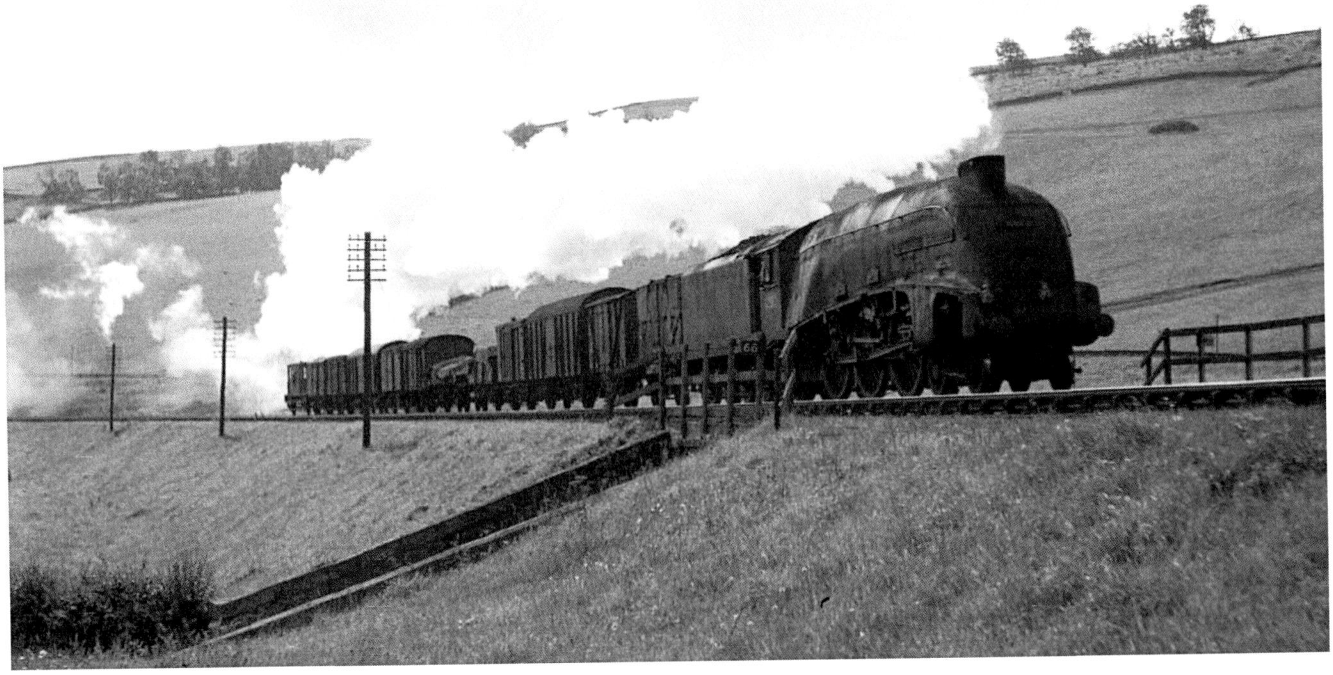

Above: A4 No 60026 *Miles Beevor* ambles past Inverkeithing on 26 June 1965 with a five-coach relief express for Edinburgh.

Above left: Gresley teak-panelled coaches are prominent in a Sunday morning excursion from King's Cross, passing Knebworth behind No 60006 *Sir Ralph Wedgwood* on 3 March 1963.

Left: On 10 September 1962, No 60012 *Commonwealth of Australia* heads a northbound Waverley Route freight near Fountainhall Junction.

Right: No 60034 *Lord Faringdon* stands over the ash pit at Aberdeen Ferryhill after working home with the 08.25 'Grampian' from Glasgow on 12 May 1966. Six A4s were on shed at the time – one of the last occasions when so many of the class were gathered together until 2013.

Above: Piles of ash, often still hot, were a hazard at many sheds. No 7023 *Penrice Castle* stands among them at Stafford Road shed, Wolverhampton, on 31 March 1963.

Below: Only the three Vale of Rheidol 2-6-2Ts of BR's steam fleet received 'corporate blue' livery and, of course, continued in service after main-line steam ended in August 1968. At the end of the day's work on 24 June 1968, the fire is thrown out of No 7 *Owain Glyndwr* at Aberystwyth.

Left: The fireman wipes his hands after cleaning the fire of J72 No 69019 at West Hartlepool on 28 April 1962. The first of these 0-6-0Ts appeared in 1898 but this particular example was one of a batch of 28 built as late as 1949-51. Standing behind is a 'modern' J94 0-6-0ST – which was built about five years before the J72!

Below: Viewed through railing posts is BR 5MT No 73110 *The Red Knight* on the ash pits at Nine Elms, 29 January 1966. Some time before the shed closed in July 1967 the battle against growing heaps of cinders was abandoned, reportedly because the ancient-looking mobile grab used for dumping ash into wagons had succumbed.

B1 4-6-0 No 61024 *Addax* and WD 2-8-0 No 90689 beside the ash disposal plant at Wakefield on 20 February 1965. The structure seems rather primitive for such a large shed but it might be regarded today as an art form – witness the Orbit tower at the London Olympics, half a century later! Another WD, No 90210 passes by on the right.

Another North Eastern Region shed on the same day as the picture opposite and once again the camera captures a named B1 and a WD together. At Hull Dairycoates, B1 No 61032 *Stembok* and WD No 90450 ease past the coaling plant – from a distance, normally the most visible feature of the largest sheds.

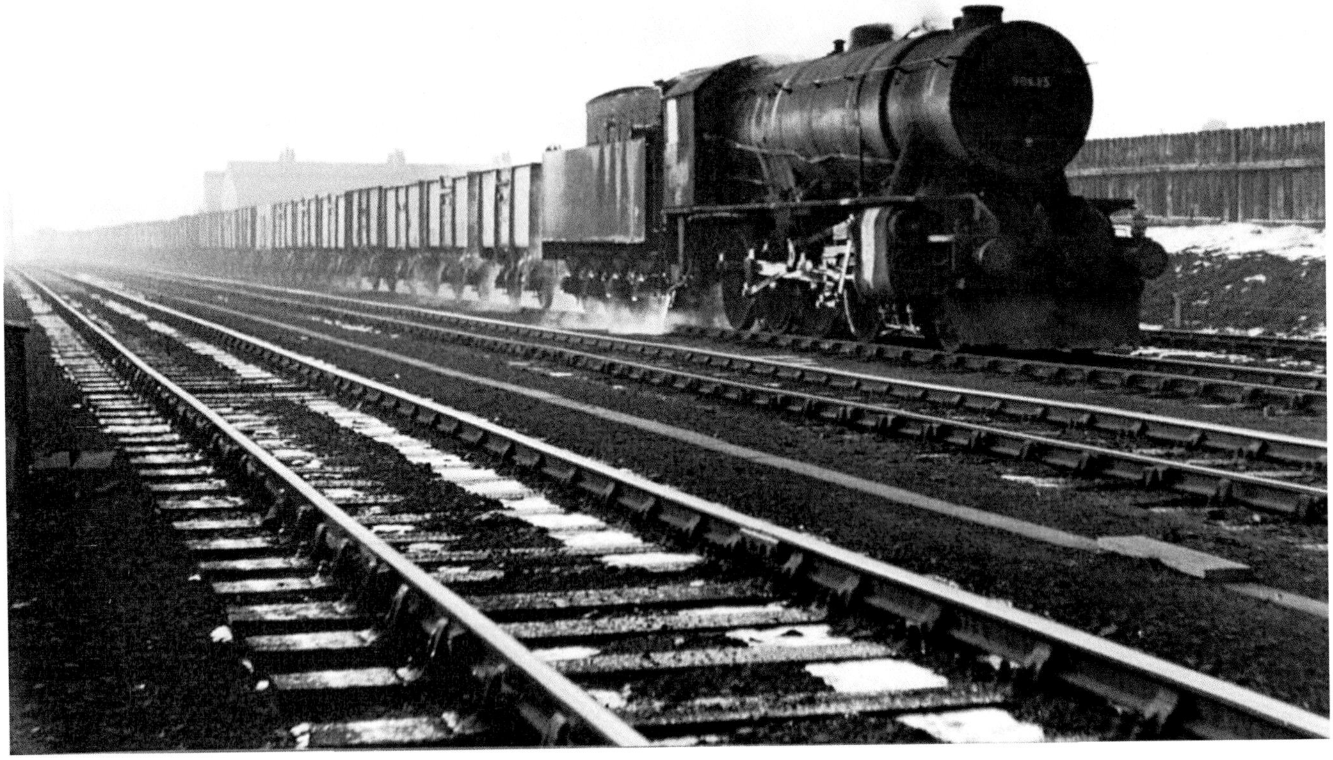

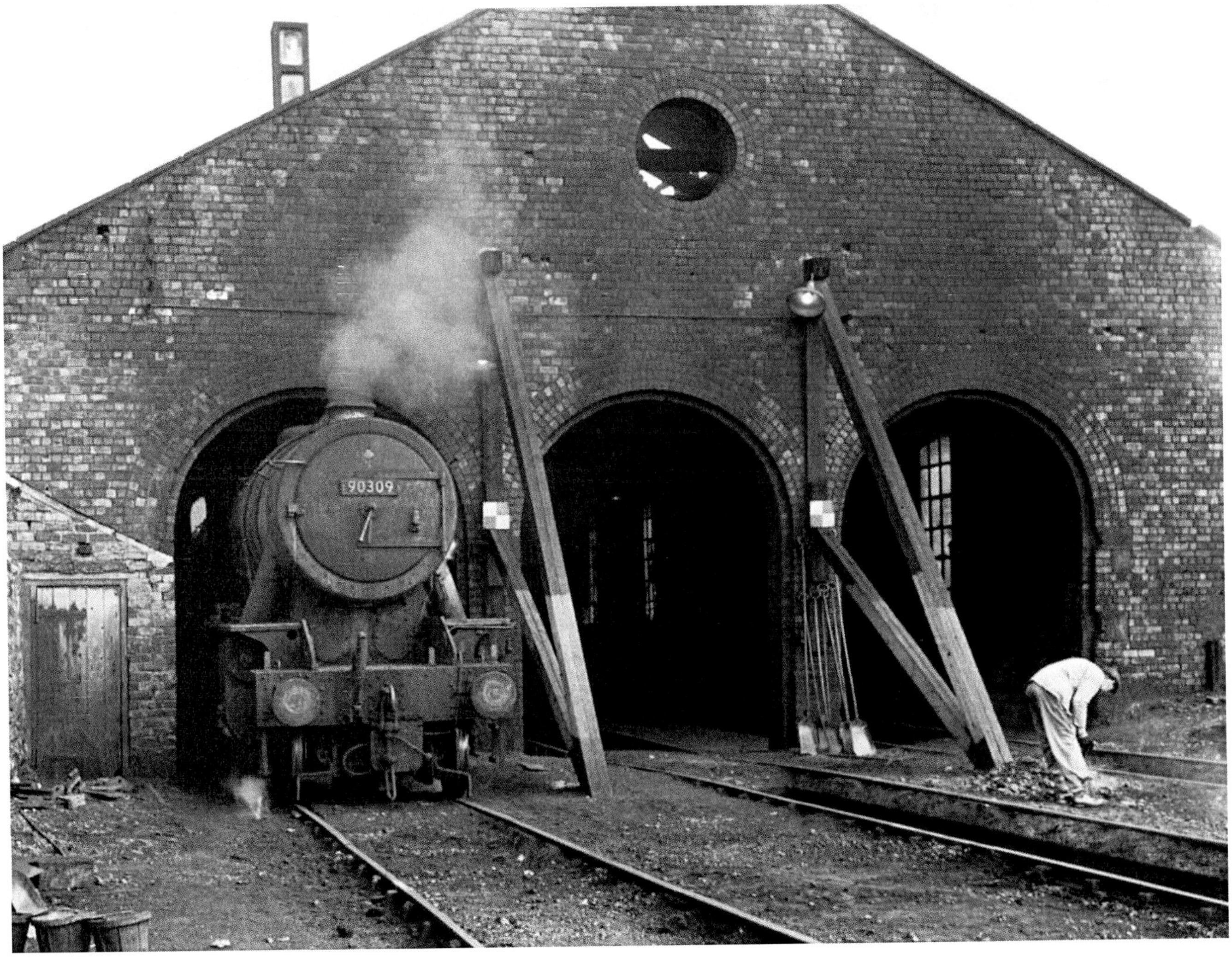
90309

Above: An up coal train passes Doncaster behind No 90156 on 10 April 1965.

Left: No 90635 heads a train of coal empties at Wakefield on 17 February 1963.

Below left: No 90309 noses out of West Hartlepool shed on 20 May 1967.

Right: No 90437 at Market Harborough on 6 June 1964.

Below: Recently ex-works and thus in unusually smart condition for a 'Dub-dee', No 90040 is at Woodford Halse shed on 3 June 1962.

52

Above left: Recently ex-works Standard 4MT No 76036 at Cricklewood shed, 16 June 1963.

Left: Fowler 2-6-4T No 42343 at Stockport Edgeley shed on 14 April 1962. The author was delighted to find such a sparkling subject on his very first 'shed-bashing' trip with a brand-new Kodak 'Sterling II' camera.

Above: Released from Darlington Works after a full overhaul, Q7 No 63471 stands at the nearby shed on 28 April 1962 awaiting its return home to Tyne Dock.

Below: The first 'Crosti' 9F to be rebuilt, three years earlier, No 92026 is at Nottingham on 21 October 1962, soon after a Heavy General overhaul at Crewe Works. 'Peak' No D156 lurks ominously in the background.

Right: Newly arrived as cover for the shed's 'Jinties', J94 No 68012 is at Westhouses on 28 May 1967 with an EE Type 1 and a BR/Sulzer Type 2. The 0-6-0ST had become redundant at Buxton when the Cromford & High Peak line closed in April.

Opposite, upper: Smoke from the lime kilns drifts above Ivatt 2MT No 46485 and BR/Sulzer Type 2 No D5137 at Hindlow on 18 February 1967.

Opposite, lower: At Langley Junction on 15 June 1963, 9F No 92149 with an up ballast train is overtaken by 'Deltic' No D9006 on the 'West Riding'.

Below: Inside the admirably smoke-free and tidy shed at Dunfermline on 22 June 1965 are WD 2-8-0s Nos 90515 and 90547, J38 0-6-0s Nos 65918 and 65921 and North British 0-4-0 shunter No D2717.

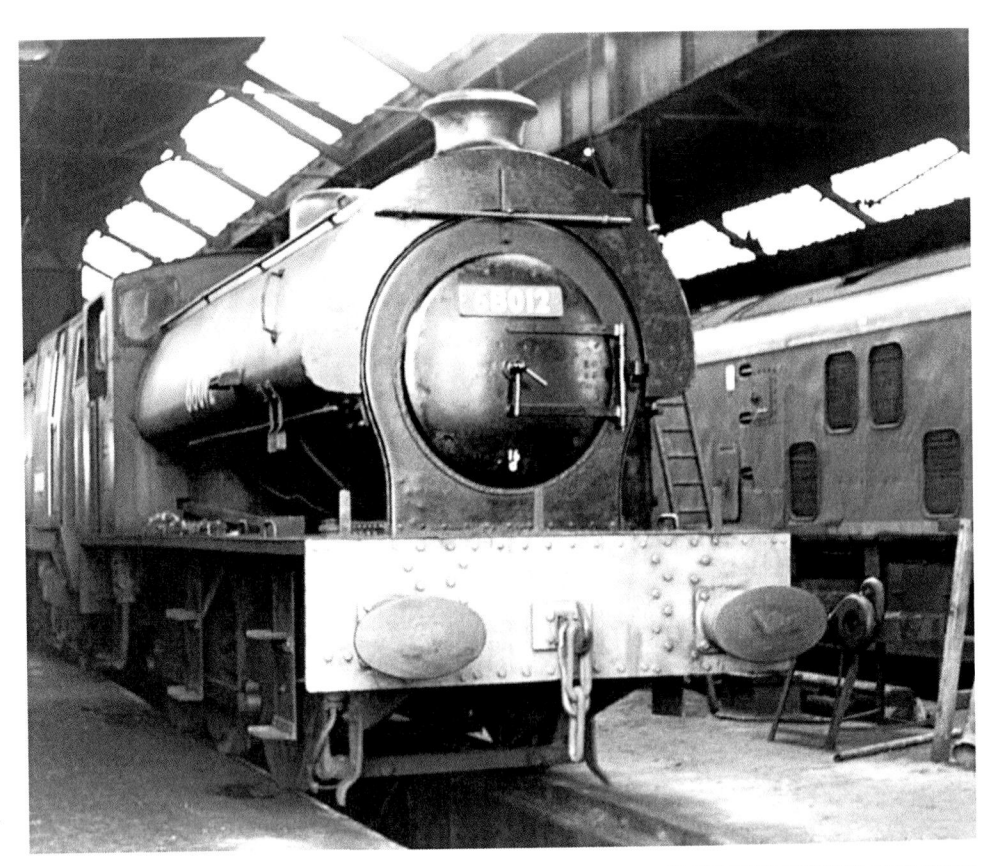

55

Above: The 9.10am King's Cross-Leeds 'White Rose' approaches Hitchin on 1 June 1963 behind A1 No 60141 *Abbotsford*.

Left: 'Black Five' No 44912 enters Leeds City with the 10.05 Bradford Forster Square-Paignton 'Devonian' on 29 September 1966.

Above: On 5 August 1965, No 7812 *Erlestoke Manor* calls at Welshpool with the up 'Cambrian Coast Express'.

Below: The down 'Bournemouth Belle', hauled by 'West Country' No 34024 *Tamar Valley*, at Micheldever on 16 June 1967, three weeks before the end of Southern Region steam.

Unrebuilt 'West Country' Pacific No 34038 *Lynton* has just been turned at Bournemouth shed on 20 May 1962 after arriving with a train from Waterloo.

At Perth shed on 15 May 1963, No 72009 *Clan Stewart* comes off the turntable, facing the right way for its homeward journey to Carlisle.

One of the less extravagantly-named
V2 2-6-2s, No 60860 *Durham School*
stands on the turntable at its home shed
of Heaton on 28 April 1962.

Returning in the late afternoon after
working the 'Dereham goods' on
7 September 1961, J17 0-6-0 No 65567
is turned at Norwich shed.

59

Above: In the Grouping era, the Great Western Railway's 0-6-0 'maids of all work' were the 120 Collett 2251s, dating from 1930. No 3210 is at Templecombe shed on 20 May 1962.

Below: Maunsell's standard 0-6-0 for the Southern Railway, the Q class was introduced as late as 1938. The first of just twenty locomotives, No 30530 stands next to BR 5MT No 73112 *Morgan le Fay* at Nine Elms shed on 24 January 1965.

Above: Immediately preceded by the similar but smaller-wheeled J38, Gresley's more versatile J39 of 1926 became the LNER standard 0-6-0. On 17 February 1963, a few weeks after the last examples of the 289-strong class were withdrawn, No 64927 awaits its fate at Wakefield shed. The absence of a J39 in the preservation world is surely the most glaring gap in the legacy of Britain's steam railways.

Below: Developed from Fowler's Midland Railway design of 1911, the LMS 4F 0-6-0 class totalled 580 locomotives. One of a small number paired with a high-sided tender, No 44599 is ex-works at Derby with 8F 2-8-0 No 48611 on 8 July 1962.

Above: Power of the 8F – the business end of No 48376 as the 2-8-0 runs past in the yard at Buxton shed on 18 February 1967.

Below: Sunset of the 8F – withdrawn during that very week, No 48468 is surrounded by coal salvaged from redundant tenders at Rose Grove on 29 February 1968. Yes, one may indeed speculate whether the shovel was re-arranged by the photographer!

Right: No 48441 attracts attention as it storms through a rainy Wigan with an up coal train on 19 February 1966.

Below right: Although two special trains ran next day, the last regular services on the Somerset & Dorset lines operated on Saturday 5 March 1966. On that day, No 48706 enters Evercreech Junction, working from Bath Green Park to Bournemouth with a Great Western Society railtour. This was one of two specials which ran on that Saturday; the other is pictured on page 65.

63

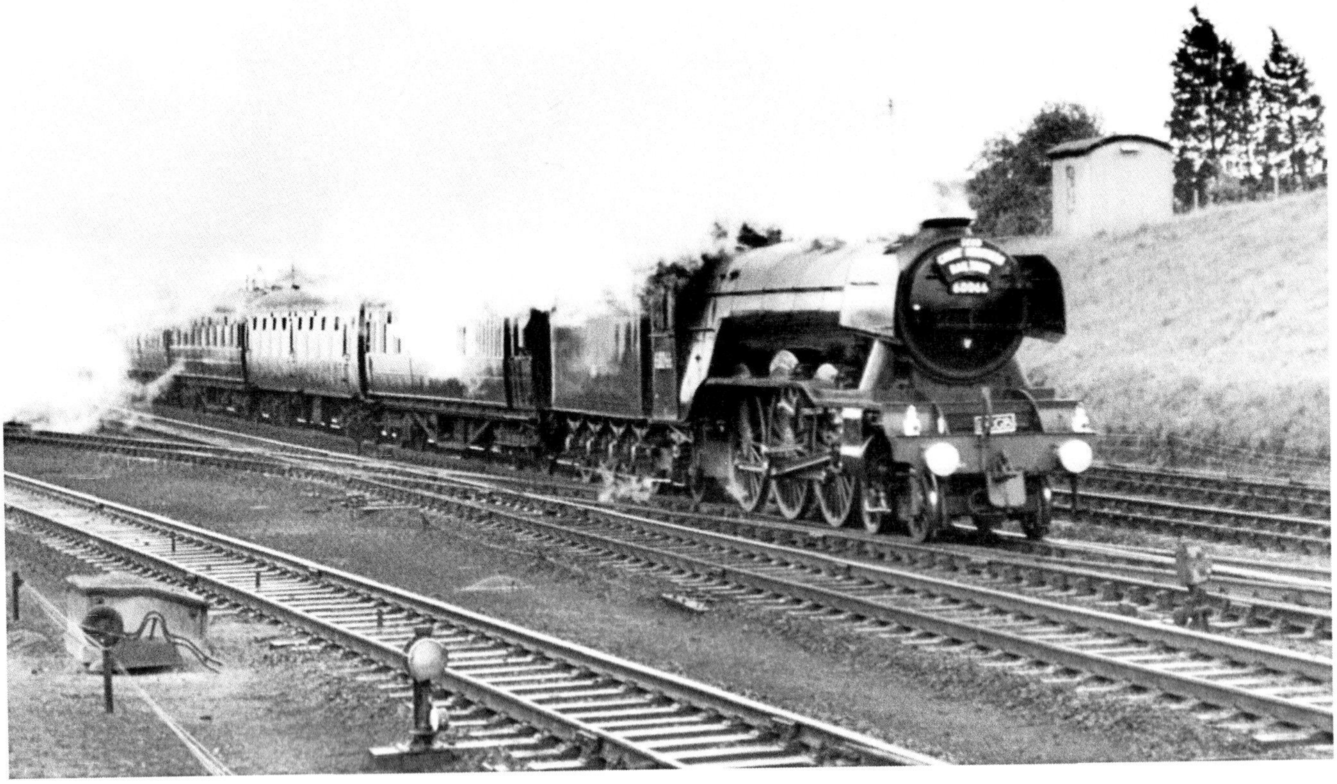

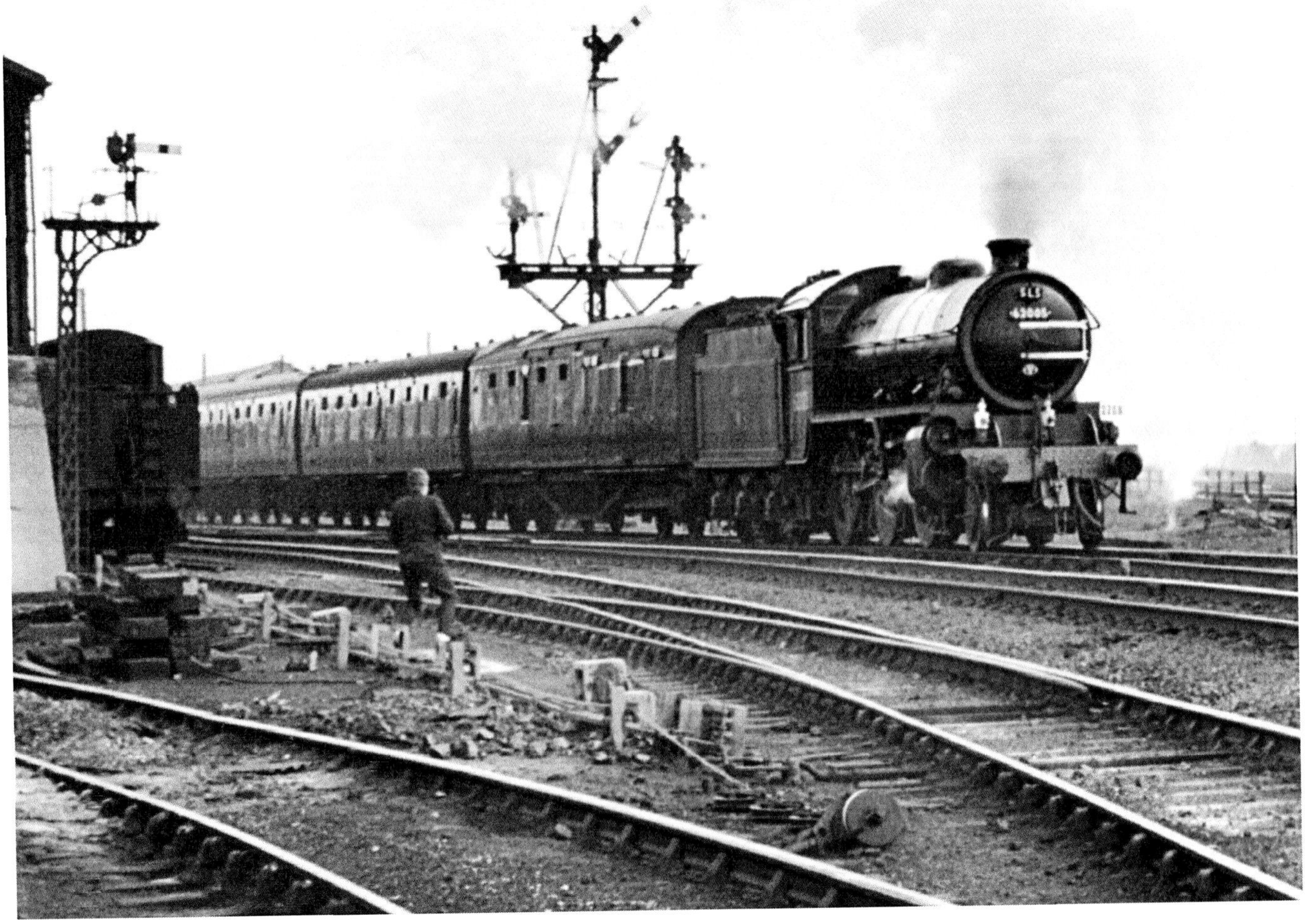

Above left: On 19 May 1962, A3 No 60066 *Merry Hampton* passes Knebworth with the Locomotive Club of Great Britain King's Cross-Doncaster 'Great Northern Rail Tour'.

Left: K1 2-6-0 No 62005 runs past West Hartlepool shed with empty stock for a Stephenson Locomotive Society railtour on 20 May 1967.

Above: Ivatt 2MT 2-6-2Ts Nos 41307 and 41249 leave Evercreech Junction for Highbridge with 'The Somerset & Dorset Rail Tour' on 5 March 1966. The Ivatt tanks had worked the LCGB special from Templecombe and on their return to Evercreech Junction from the Highbridge branch they handed over the train to a pair of unrebuilt Bulleid Pacifics.

Above: Stanier 8F 2-8-0 No 48141 pulls away from Wigan North Western and heads down the West Coast main line with a rake of coal wagons on 19 February 1966.

Above right: The fireman of K1 No 62057 is clearly filling the firebox on 5 November 1966 as the 2-6-0 gets ready to set off from the yards at North Blyth with a coal train.

Right: Acrid smoke rolls across Basingstoke as 'West Country' No 34015 *Exmouth* starts a London-bound train of parcels vans from the yards west of the station on 22 November 1966.

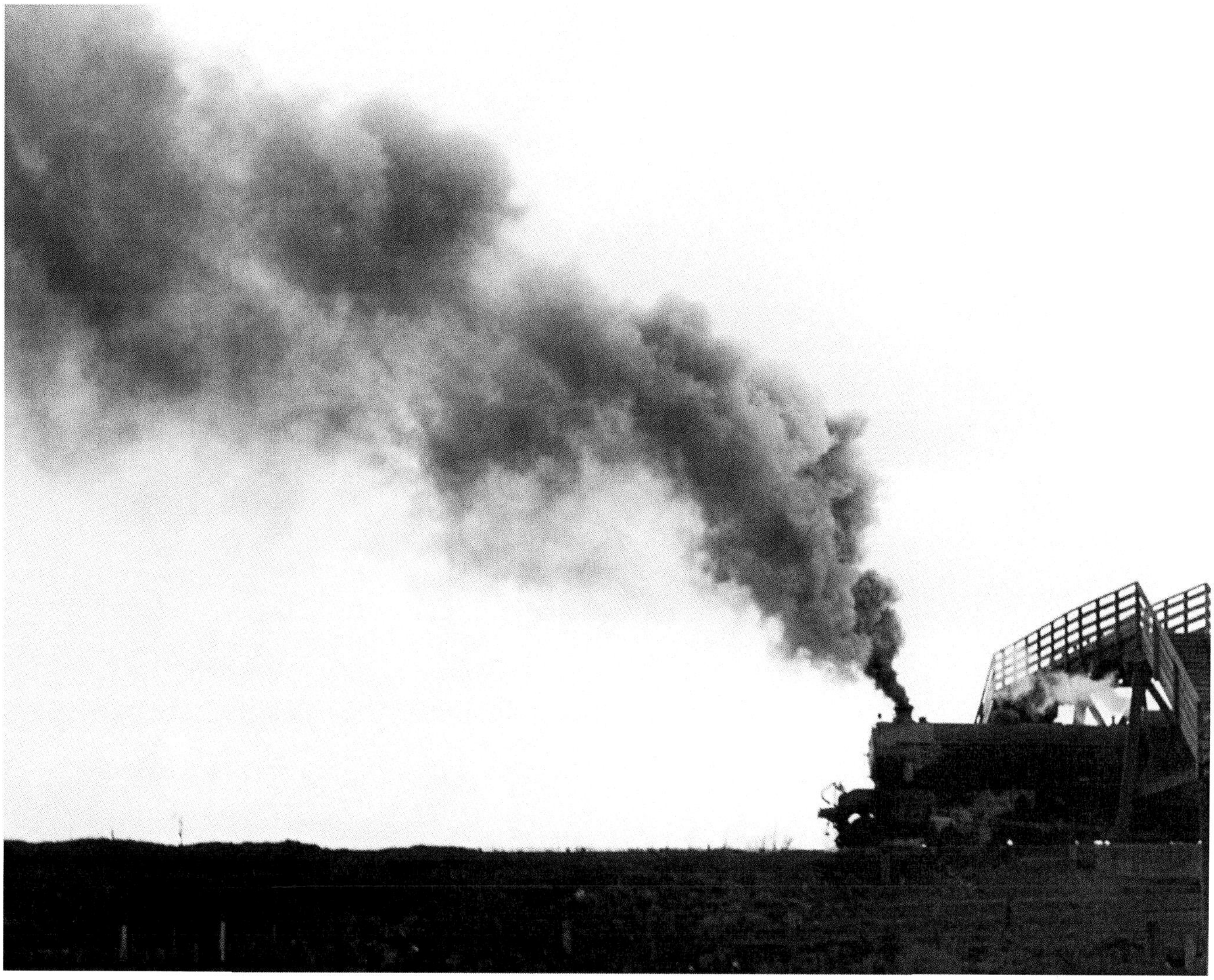

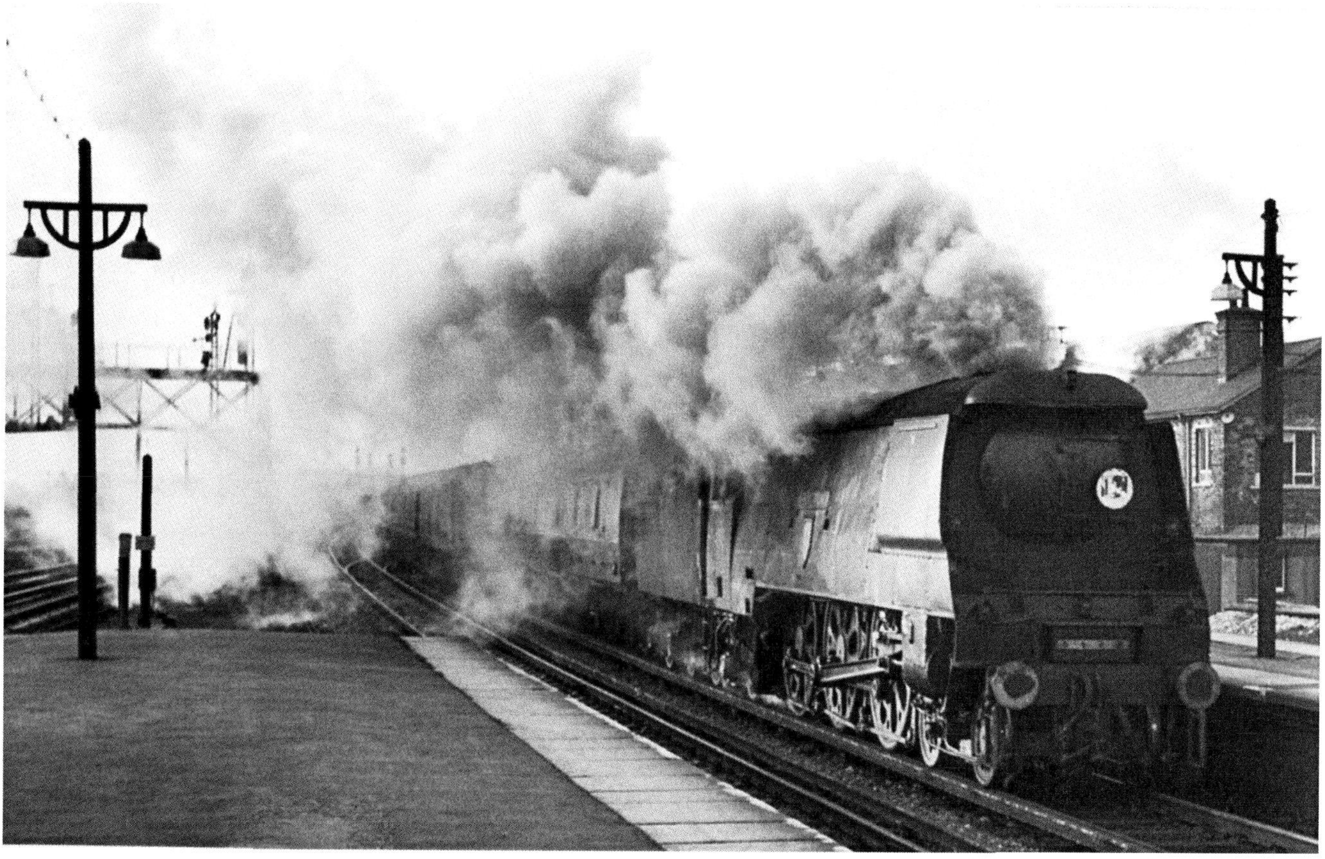

Left: Running-in on a down parcels working, 'Castle' No 5078 *Beaufort* reverses back to its train after detaching vans at Reading on 16 April 1961.

Right: BR 4MT 2-6-0 No 76065 heads a down evening parcels in the long cutting approaching Weybridge on 26 July 1965.

Below right: Leaving Blyth with a short parcels train on 28 April 1962 is V1 2-6-2T No 67641.

Below: 'Britannia' Pacific No 70050 *Firth of Clyde* at Glasgow St.Enoch after arriving with a parcels train on 11 May 1966.

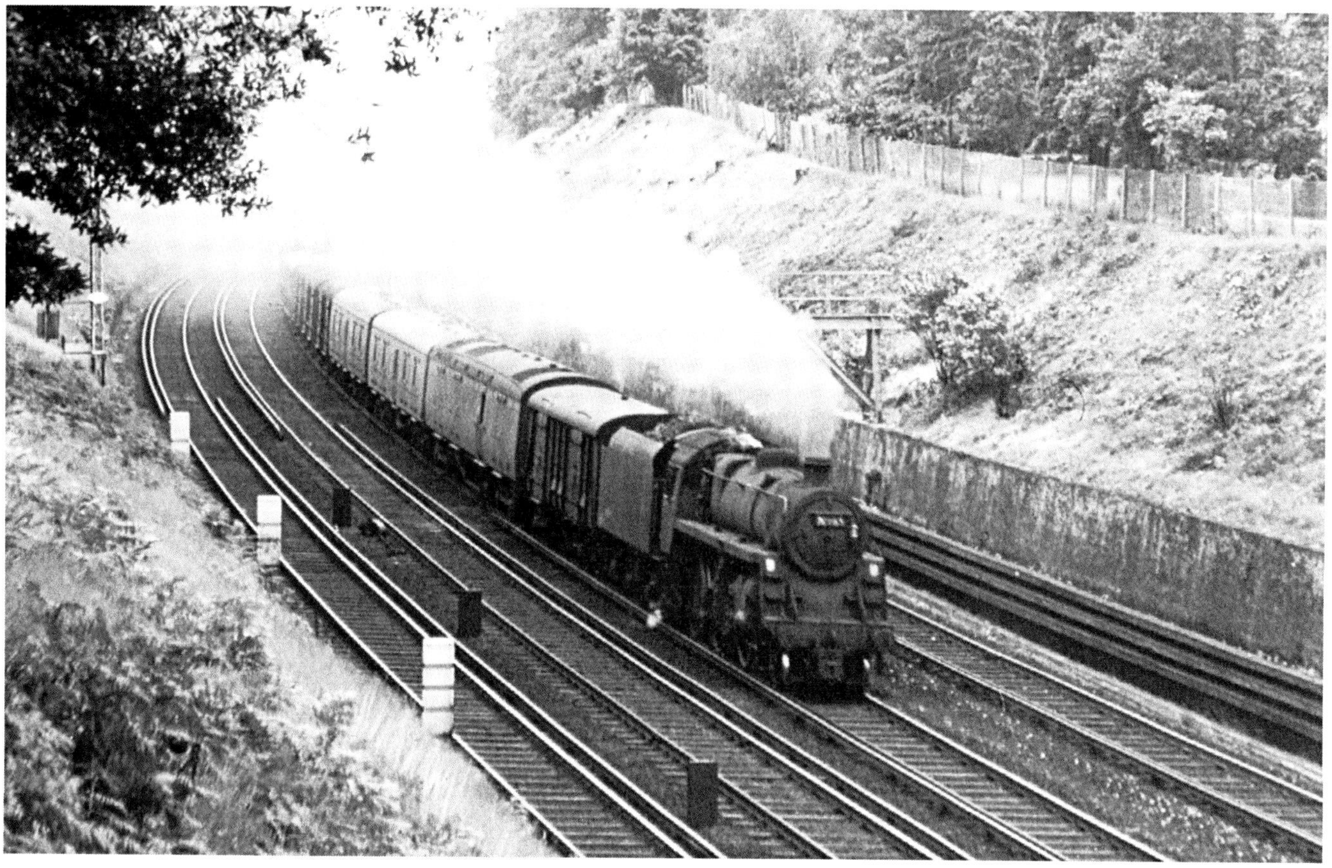

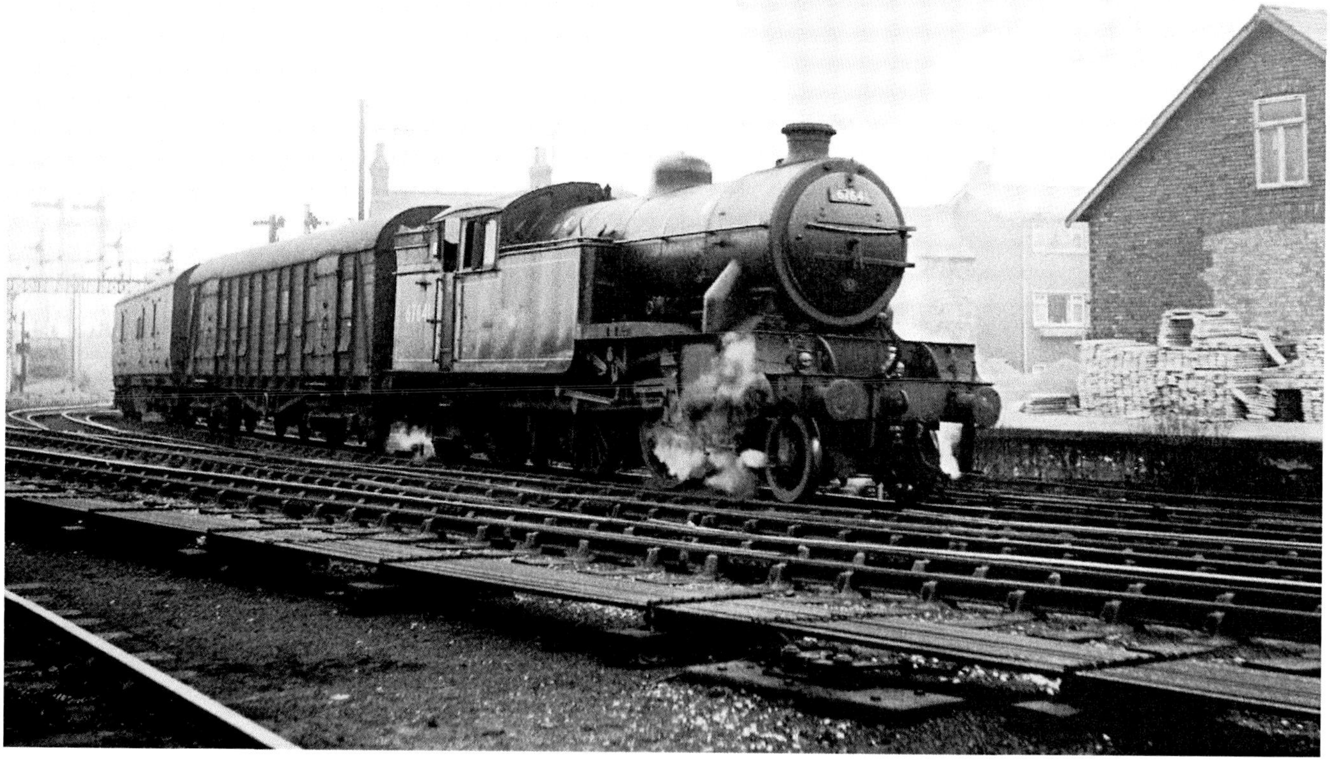

Above: Stanier's 4MT 2-6-4T was a taper-boiler development of the Fowler design illustrated on page 52. Although both had been withdrawn in June, Nos 42587 and 42665 remain at Low Moor shed on 8 October 1967.

Right: Unlike other large six-coupled tank engines, the W 2-6-4T was mainly used for freight working. In the yard of Norwood Junction shed on 7 December 1963 is No 31912.

Below: The 7200 2-8-2Ts were originally 4200 2-8-0Ts, but were rebuilt with larger bunkers from 1934 onwards and renumbered. On 26 August 1962, No 7242 is at Radyr shed where several were based along with 5600 0-6-2Ts, among them No 6635 which is standing nearby.

BR 4MT 2-6-4T No 80124 shares St.Margaret's shed on 10 May 1966 with types representing two pre-Nationalisation companies. The LMS 2-6-4T on the right is Fairburn 4MT No 42128 and in the background is LNER V2 No 60824.

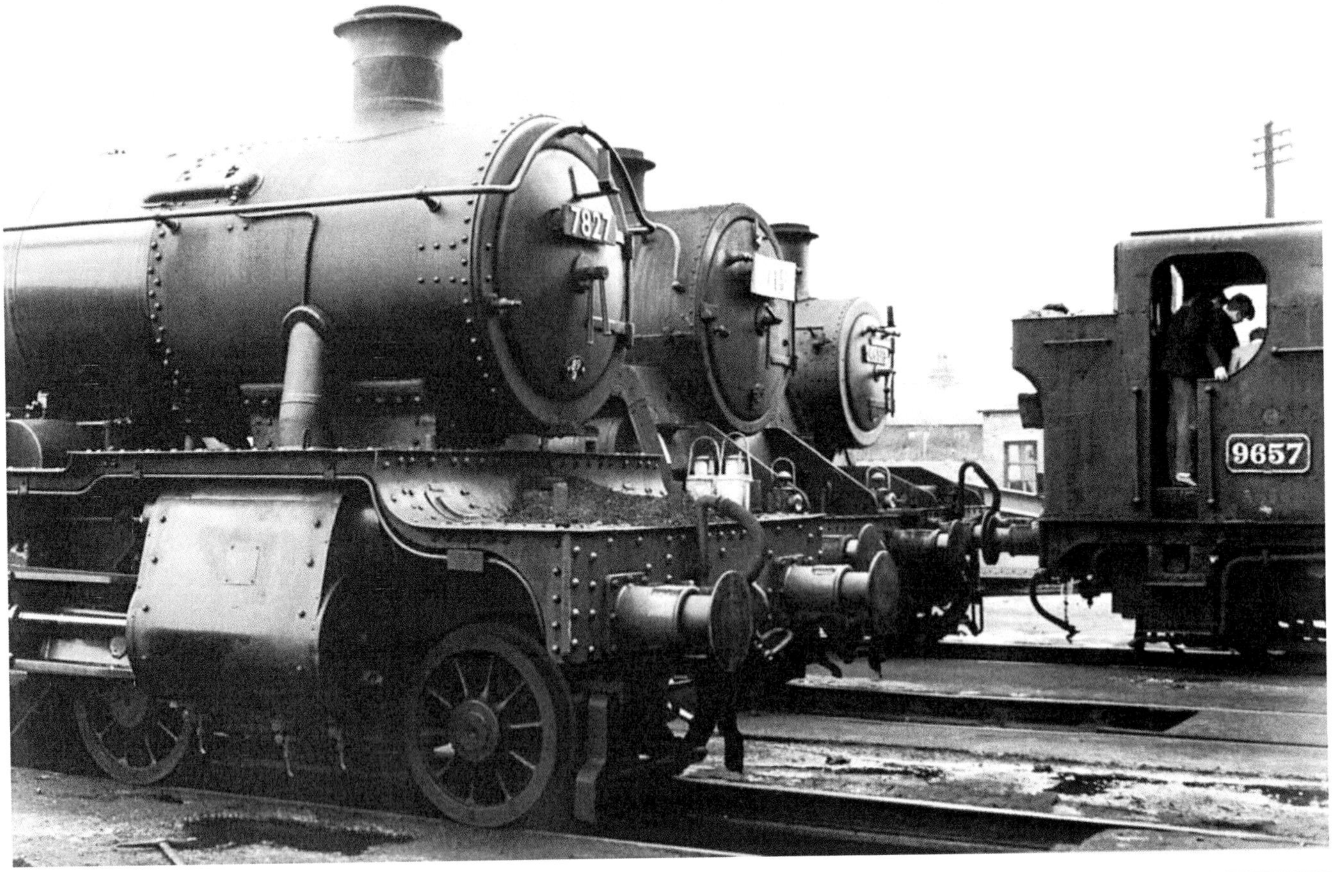
7827
9657

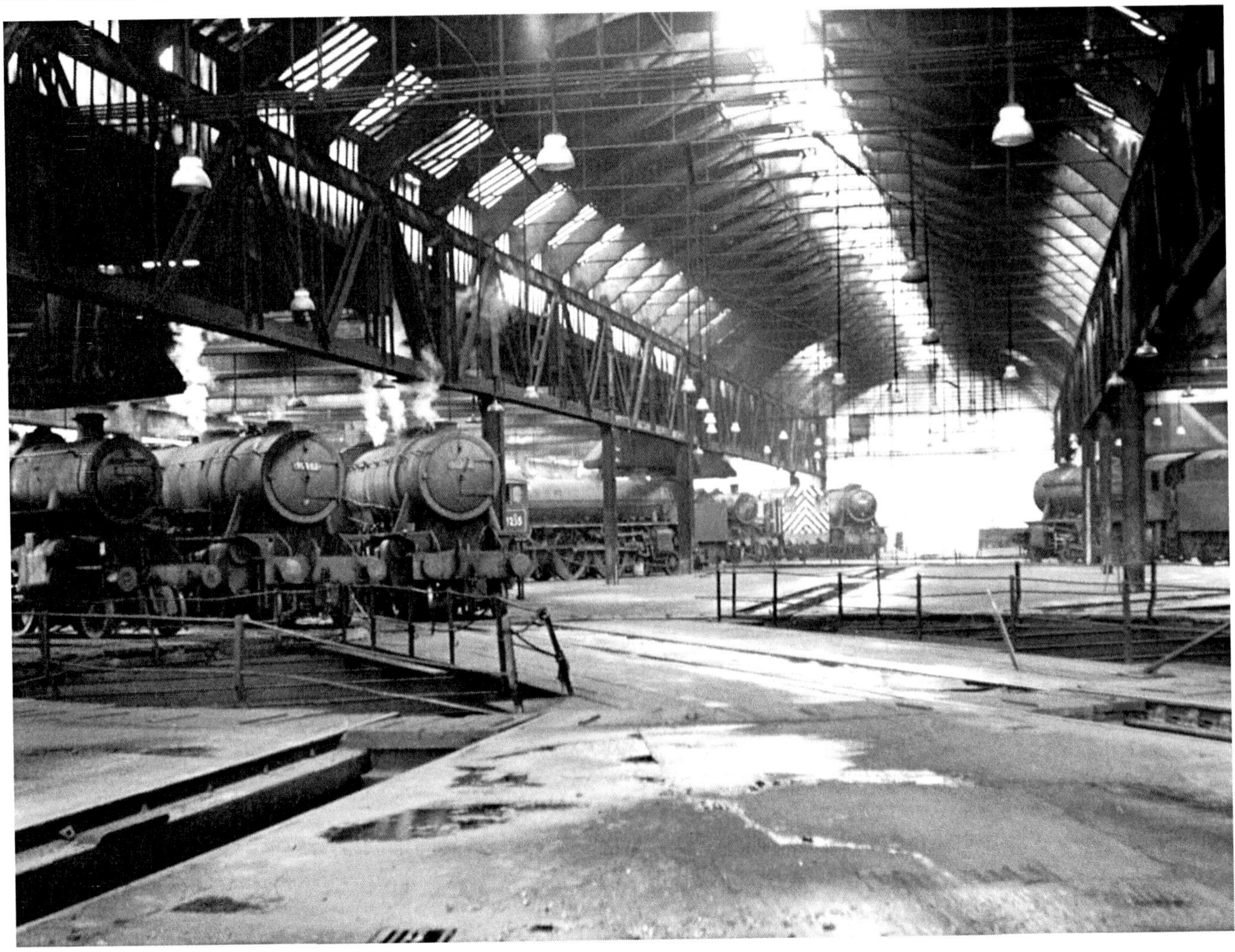

Left: Great Western, BR and LMS types at Oswestry shed on 21 April 1963. No 7827 *Lydham Manor*, Standard 5MT No 73030 and Ivatt 2MT No 46513 (all three built in BR days!) stand side by side while 5700 0-6-0PT No 9657 is 'cabbed' by enthusiasts.

Left: In the roundhouse at Hull Dairycoates on 20 February 1965 are some of the shed's generous allocation of WD 2-8-0s, including Nos 90352, 90272, 90462 and (on the right) 90009. Ivatt 4MTs Nos 43078 and 43079 represent the LMS and the sole LNER presence is B1 4-6-0 No 61255.

Above: Examples of LMS, Great Central and BR Standard designs at Langwith Junction on 2 October 1965 – Stanier 5MT 4-6-0 No 45289, O4 2-8-0 No 63843 and 9F 2-10-0 No 92145.

Below: Locomotives from several BR regions frequently met at Woodford Halse shed and, on 16 December 1962, these five each have a different genesis. LMS 8F No 48293, GWR 'Modified Hall' No 7925 *Westol Hall* and WD 2-8-0 No 90237 are prominent. Facing the 4-6-0 is LNER V2 No 60864 and visible above the WD's cylinder is the smokebox number of BR Standard 'Britannia' No 70051 *Firth of Forth*.

74

Above: H 0-4-4T No 31005 at Three Bridges on 23 September 1962. The BR tender belongs to Standard 4MT 4-6-0 No 75078 and still sporting the early BR emblem is the tender of a Q1 0-6-0.

Above left: USA 0-6-0T No 30072, the shed pilot at Guildford, on 14 January 1967. Steam drifting in the still air hides the identity of Standard 4MT 2-6-0 No 76031.

Left: Standing next to BR 3MT 2-6-2T No 82026 at Nine Elms on 24 January 1965 is 'Battle of Britain' No 34051 *Winston Churchill*. The former Prime Minister died on this day and, six days later, No 34051 hauled his funeral train from Waterloo to Handborough.

Right: No 35026 *Lamport & Holt Line* has arrived at Bournemouth Central with the 08.25 from Waterloo (a relief to the 08.30) on 4 June 1966. Alongside, the seemingly camera-shy No 76031 is again wreathed in steam.

75

Heading the 18.05 Waterloo-Basingstoke
on 6 July 1962, BR Standard 5MT No 73116 *Iseult*
gathers speed past Queens Road Battersea, where
U 2-6-0 No 31625 is waiting for the road into the
terminus with empty stock from Clapham Junction.

BR 3MT No 77018 sets off from Ayr on 13 May 1966 with the 17.08 to Kilmarnock, formed of a Royal Mail TPO van and BR and LMS non-gangwayed stock. Coupled to 4MT 2-6-0 No 76101 is one of the last few LNER-designed non-gangwayed coaches still in service at that time.

Standard 5MT 4-6-0 No 73067 with Standard 4MT 4-6-0s
Nos 75006 and 75071 at Shrewsbury shed on 7 August 1965,
in the company of a 'Manor' and an Ivatt 2MT 2-6-0.

BR Standard 4MT 4-6-0 No 75002 at Portmadoc (the contemporary spelling) with an up freight on 12 August 1966.

BR Standard 4MT 2-6-0 No 76014 at Evercreech Junction with the 13.10 Bournemouth-Bristol on 6 November 1965.

80

Above left: No 34044 *Woolacombe* leaves Templecombe with the 09.37 Bournemouth-Bath Green Park on 6 November 1965.

Left: Passing beneath the L&SW line, the 11.41 Bournemouth-Bristol calls at Templecombe's low level S&D platform on 6 November 1965 for BR 4MT 4-6-0 No 75072 to change crew.

Above: Ivatt 2-6-2T No 41307 at Evercreech Junction with the 14.18 Highbridge-Templecombe, 6 November 1965.

Below: The now-preserved S&D 7F 2-8-0 No 53808 at Weymouth before departing for Bath Green Park at the head of an Ian Allan railtour on 22 September 1962.

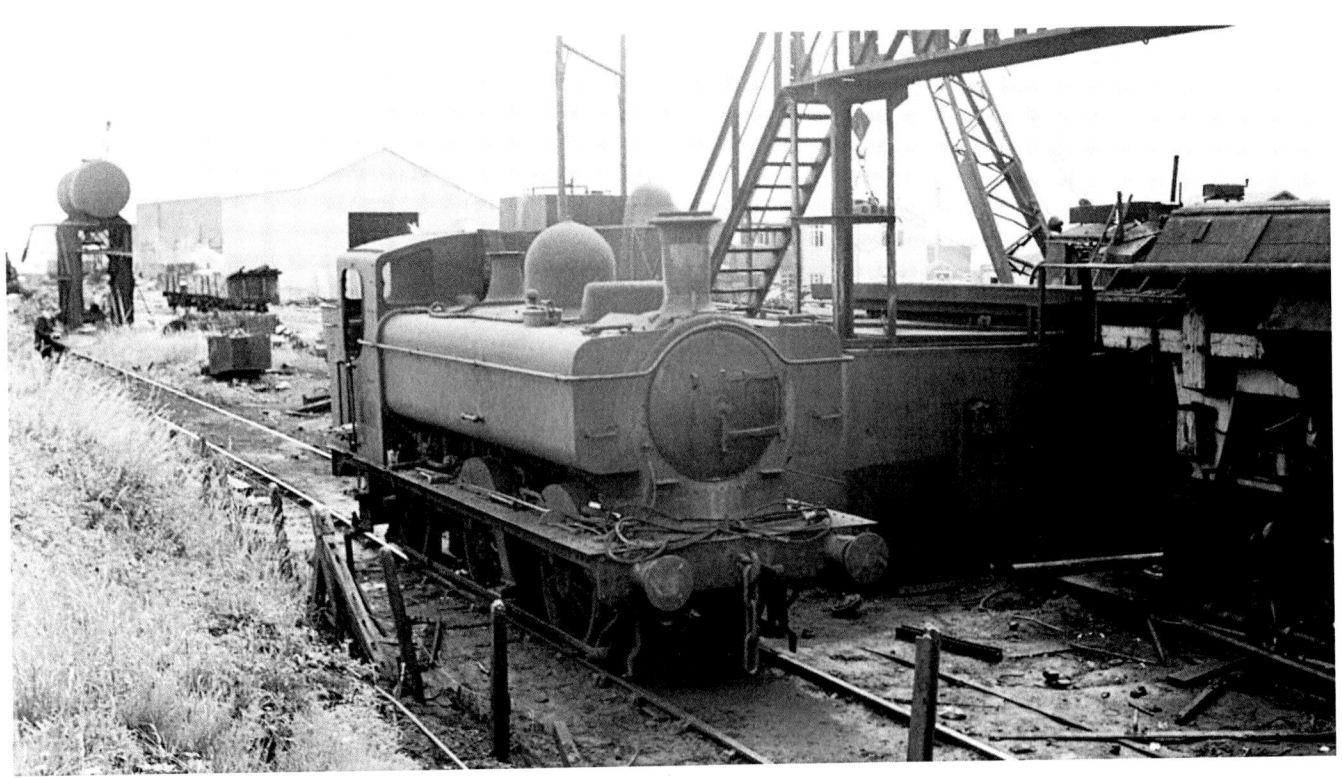

Above: 'Pannier' No 9642 in the Bridgend yard of R S Hayes on 9 July 1967. The 5700 was sold to the scrap metal company upon withdrawal in January 1965 and for a while was used for shunting in the yard. It went for preservation in 1968.

Below: 8F No 48151 heads north from Carnforth on 17 October 1967 with a train of hopper wagons. Coal from the tender of withdrawn Standard 4MT No 75058, in the yard of the shed, has been emptied into the wagon standing alongside.

Right: A Portsmouth Harbour-Waterloo service, formed of 'Pompey' units, approaches as No 34101 *Hartland* restarts the 8.35am Waterloo-Bournemouth semi-fast from its stop at Surbiton on 24 June 1963.

Below: Q6 0-8-0 No 63395 takes a load of 21-ton mineral wagons through Pelaw, heading towards Sunderland, on 5 November 1966.

Above: At dusk on 24 August 1967, 8F No 48664 hurries south at Royston & Notton with empty coal wagons.

Below: Southbound coal empties pass Ayr shed behind 'Crab' 2-6-0 No 42803 on 15 September 1962.

Below: No 92109 drifts past Heswall Hills on 21 August 1967 with empty Summers iron ore hoppers returning to Bidston.

Bottom: A down coal train hauled by J27 No 65860 runs beside the sea near Ryhope on 20 May 1967.

Above: With the same down evening parcels working as that pictured at the top of page 69, S15 4-6-0 No 30837 speeds along the embankment south of Weybridge on 12 April 1965.

Right: BR Standard 5MT 4-6-0 No 73065 at Nine Elms shed on 14 January 1967.

Opposite, upper: 9F No 92004 climbs from Ince Moss Junction to pass above the West Coast main line south of Wigan with an eastbound train of 21-ton hoppers on 25 March 1967. Long gone today, the slag tips behind the 9F and its train were known as the 'Wigan Alps'.

Opposite, lower: Ivatt 2MT 2-6-2T No 41202 is the Stockport Edgeley station pilot on 16 March 1966.

87

Above: Stanier 8F 2-8-0 No 48110 takes a southbound coal train past the shed and through the station at Stafford on 16 March 1966.

Below: Standard 2-6-4T No 80045 at Glasgow Central with the 15.57 to Gourock on 11 May 1966.

Right: On 17 October 1967, 'Black Five' No 44926 shunts oil wagons into the yards near the entrance to Edge Hill shed. The street sign on the house reads 'Tiverton Street' – from which (quoting the ubiquitous phrase in Aidan Fuller's invaluable and fondly-remembered *British Locomotive Shed Directory*) "a cinder path leads to the shed".

Below right: J15 0-6-0 No 65476 at Chingford on 7 April 1962 with the Locomotive Club of Great Britain 'Great Eastern Suburban Rail Tour'.

Above: The fireman of No 60016 *Silver King* keeps an eye on enthusiasts visiting St.Rollox shed in Glasgow on 3 April 1964 as the A4 reverses past. Taking water outside the running shed is A2 No 60535 *Hornet's Beauty*.

Below: The 16.20 Hull-Doncaster has reached its destination on 10 April 1965 behind No 61360 and the B1's number is checked in the book.

Right: On 23 March 1968, participants on 'The Bronte' railtour photograph the locomotive during a water stop at Leicester. Hauled by *Flying Scotsman*, the train ran from St.Pancras to Keighley and back to King's Cross.

Right: Young spotters near the Etterby Road bridge, south of Kingmoor shed, watch Stanier 5MT No 44761 cross the River Eden with an up parcels train and head towards Carlisle on 22 August 1967.

91

Right: The man who saved A3 No 4472 *Flying Scotsman* in 1963, Alan Pegler stands on his locomotive's second tender to supervise watering at Leicester during 'The Bronte' railtour of 23 March 1968.

Below right: Opening the Audley End Miniature Railway on 16 May 1964, motor racing driver Stirling Moss looks confidently in command of the 10¼ in gauge line's steam locomotive, a 1948-built Curwen & Newbery 4-4-2.

Below: The best-known 'Top Shed' driver of his generation, Bill Hoole retired in 1959, ending his association with A4 No 60007 *Sir Nigel Gresley*. He then moved to North Wales, to work on the Festiniog Railway where 1863-built 0-4-0ST *Prince* became his somewhat smaller regular locomotive; he is on the footplate at Tan-y-Bwlch on 1 May 1965.

Left: Artist and locomotive owner David Shepherd chats from the fireman's seat of No 75029 during the last Open Day at the Longmoor Military Railway, on 5 July 1969. He had purchased the Standard 4MT, along with 9F No 92203, in 1968 and the two locomotives were based at Longmoor for a few years until the East Somerset Railway opened.

Below: The driver of 1937-built Hudswell Clark 0-4-0ST No 1672, based at Stuart Street power station, Manchester, points out his next move to photographer Colin Gifford on 12 August 1968 – the day after the 'Fifteen Guinea Special'. Colin was already an enthusiastic photographer of the industrial scene and, from this day onwards, more people would turn to recording the steam railways of British industry.

Above: A Yorkshire Engine Co saddle-tank operated by the steelworks takes a rake of hopper and mineral wagons across the swing bridge at Workington on 22 August 1967.

Below: A Hunslet 0-6-0ST dating from the early 1950s shunts at Scunthorpe on 15 June 1968.

The view from a convenient road bridge near the blast furnaces at Stewarts & Lloyds' steelworks in Corby on 6 September 1968, with Hawthorn Leslie 0-6-0ST No 13 carefully manoeuvring its load.

Above: No 1012 *County of Denbigh* and a 'Hall', both withdrawn, at Swindon Works on 27 September 1964. BR 5MT No 73012 is in store just prior to withdrawal.

Below: The bodies of Sentinels Y1 No 68149 and Y3 No 68180 (withdrawn in January 1958 and May 1956, respectively) in use as tool stores at Darlington North Road scrapyard, 3 October 1964.

Above: Almost three and a half years after withdrawal – and before its brush with oblivion in South Wales – No 71000 *Duke of Gloucester* is at Crewe Works on 3 April 1966.

Right: A tranquil scene at BR's smallest main workshops – Ryde Works on 26 August 1964.

Below: Withdrawn motive power from vastly different eras of British railway history at Darlington Works on 3 October 1964. After withdrawal in April 1962, J21 0-6-0 No 65033 survived precariously for several years before eventual preservation at Beamish Open Air Museum. Behind the J21 is partly-dismantled A4 No 60011 *Empire of India*, with its tender standing next to North British 200hp 0-4-0 diesel shunter No D2700.

97

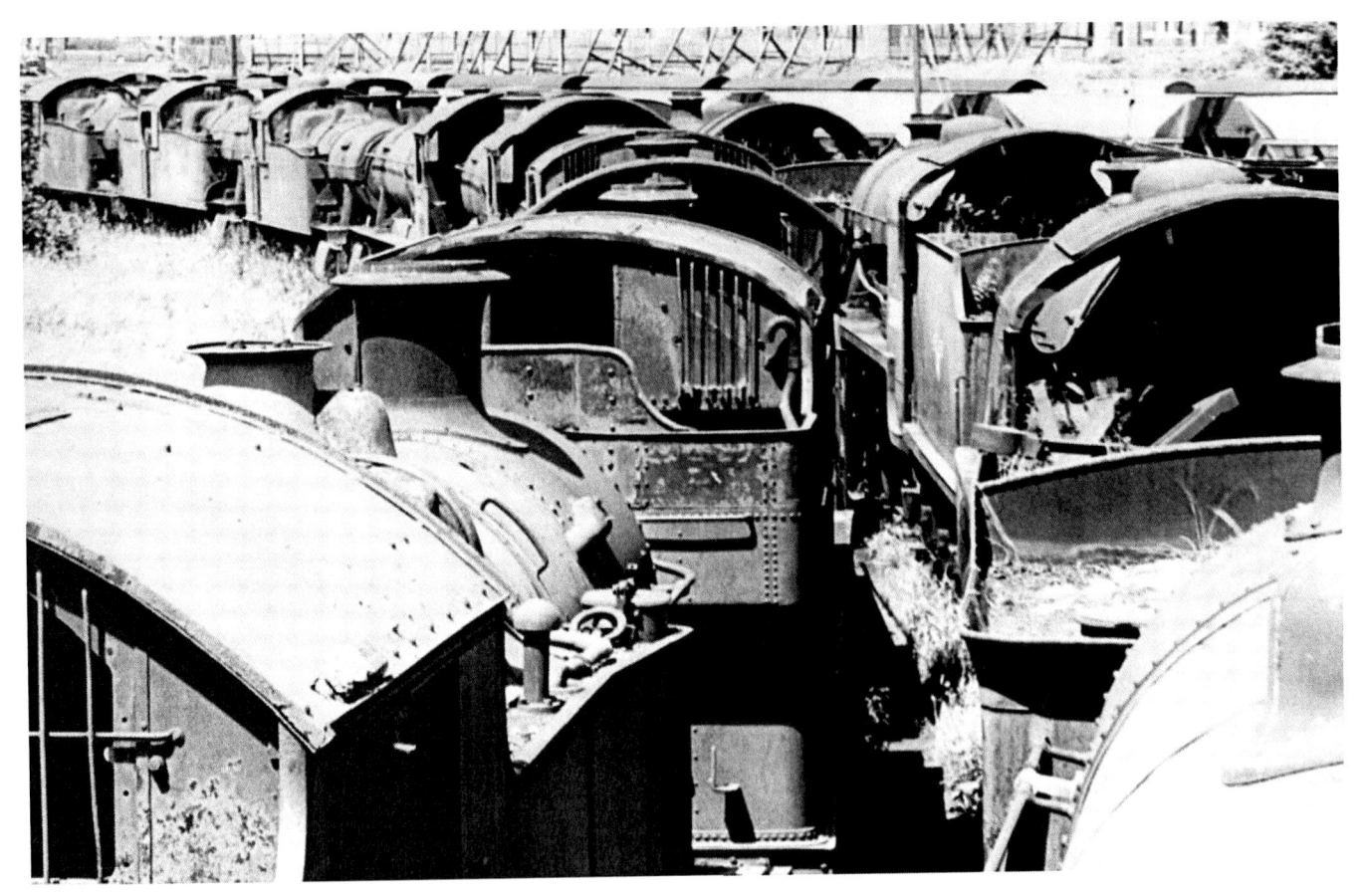

Above: Great Western locomotives, mostly tank engines, and Southern S15 4-6-0s at Dai Woodham's Barry scrapyard on 9 July 1967.

Below: The unusual outside framing of a 'King' bogie's leading axle – No 6023 *King Edward II* at Barry on 14 July 1968.

Above right: Nature finds a place on the footplate of 2-8-0 No 2874, 14 July 1968.

Right: At the end of the BR steam era, just over 200 locomotives were rusting away at Barry. 'Jubilee' No 45690 *Leander* stands in line with three 'Halls' on 14 July 1968.

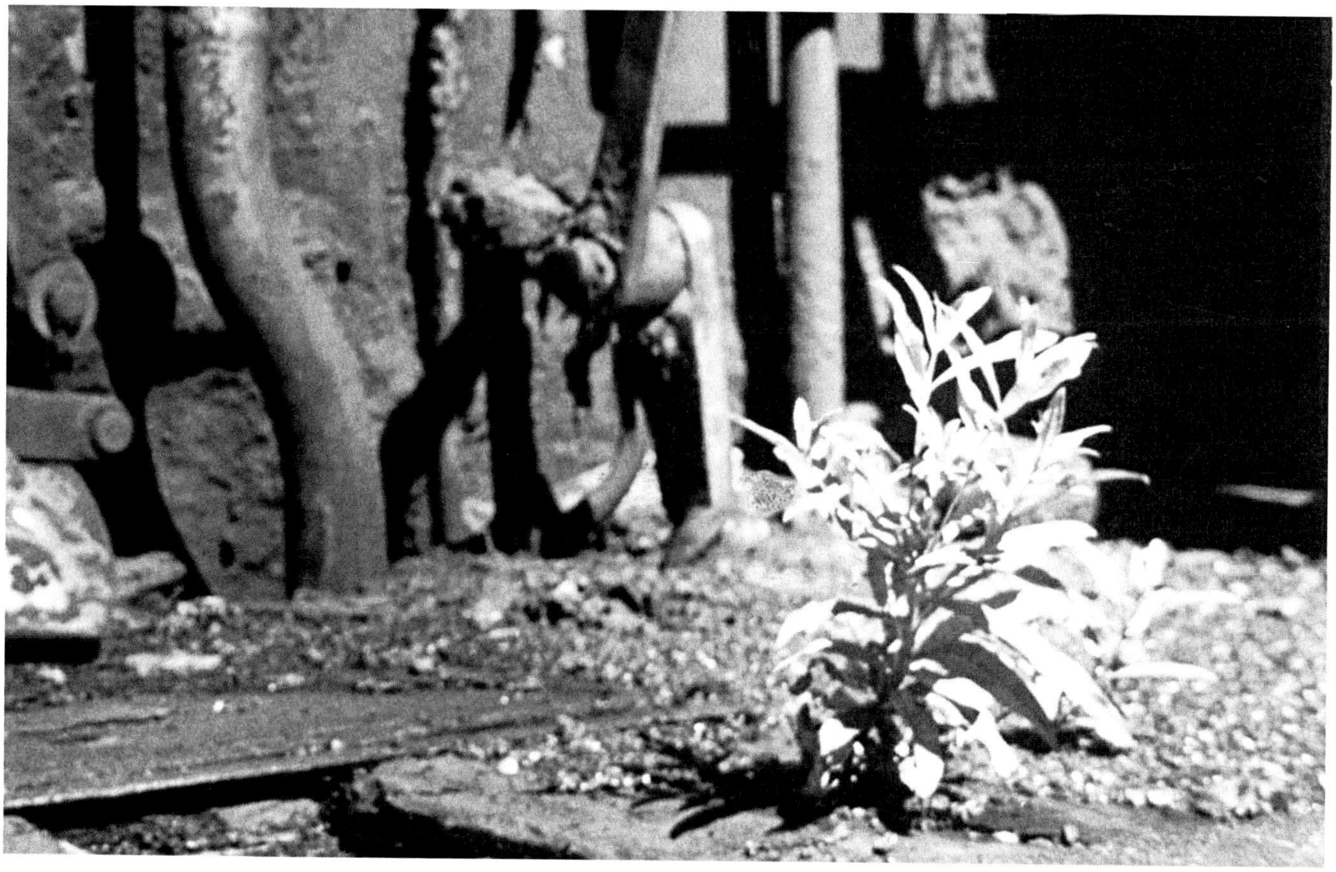

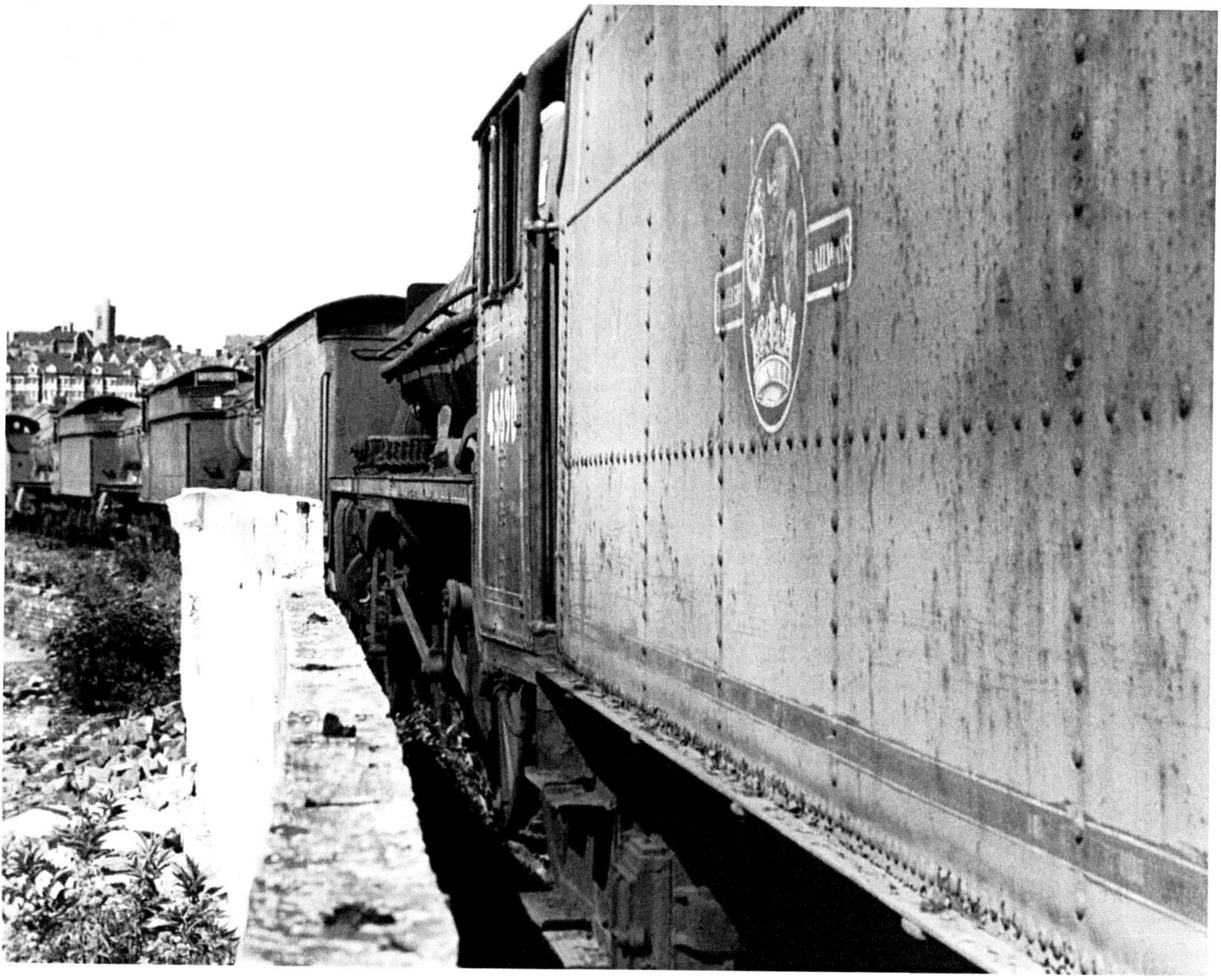

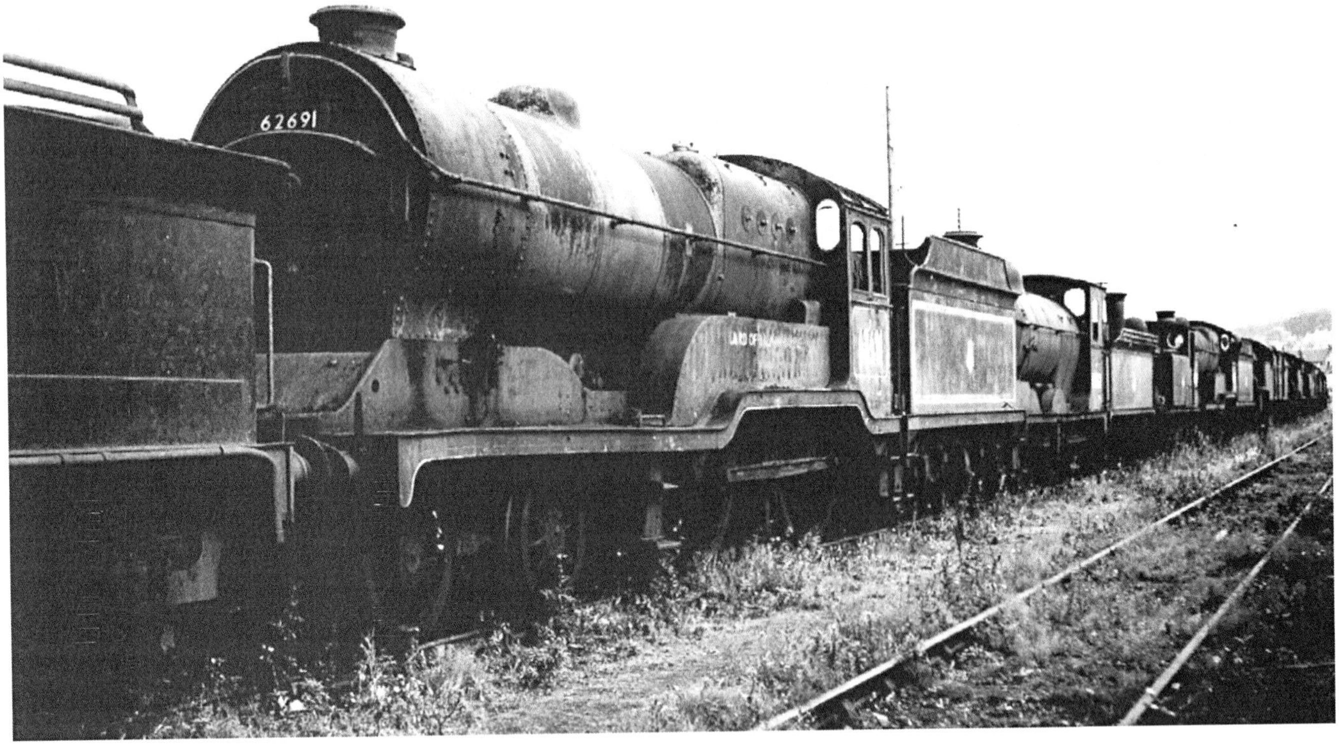
62691

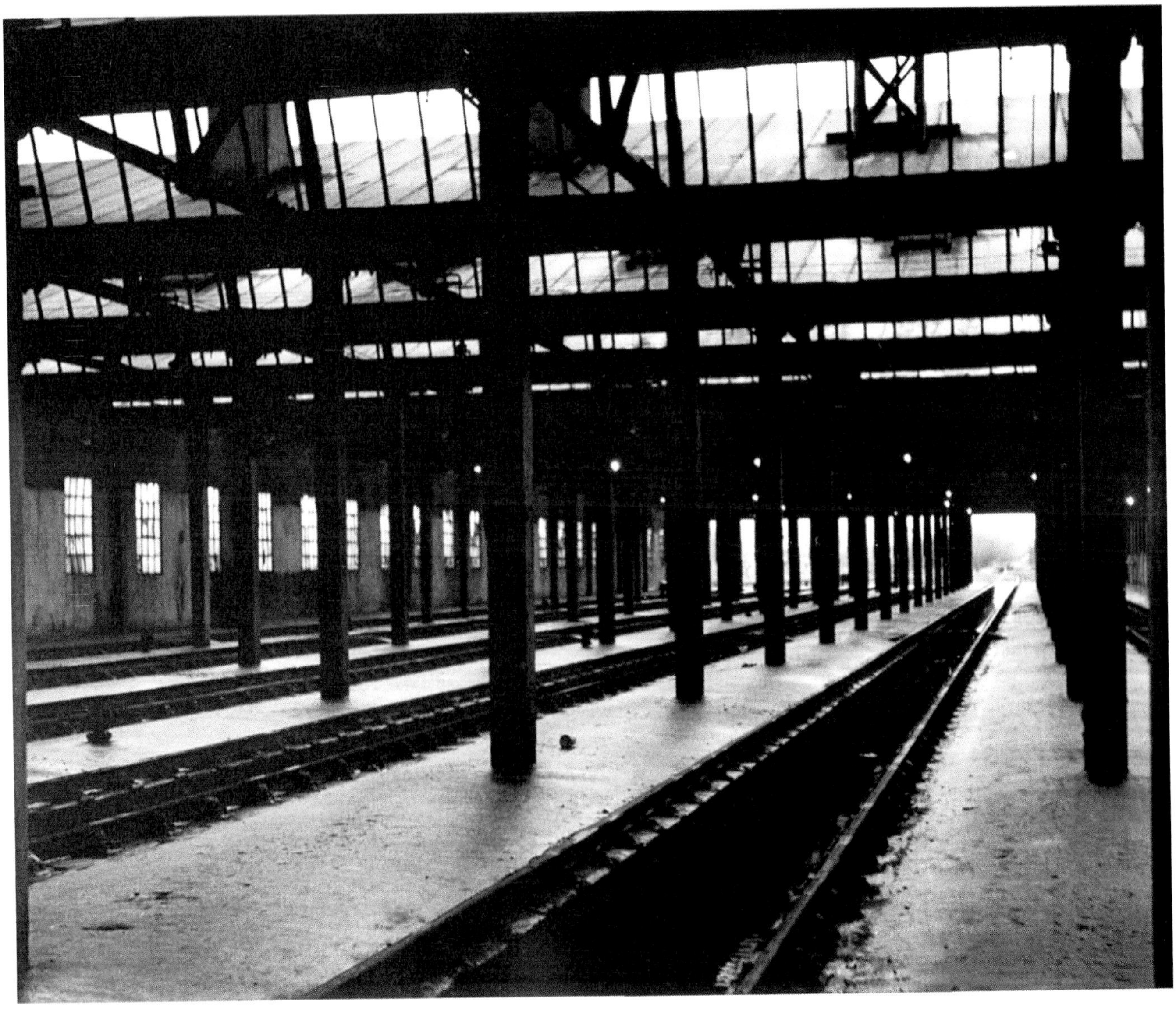

Left: One of the 'dumps' of withdrawn steam traction which grew up in the early 1960s was at Bo'ness. Among the 46 locomotives there on 10 September 1962 are D11 No 62691 *Laird of Balmawhapple*, J35 No 64532, J83 No 68448, D11 No 62693 *Roderick Dhu* and several V3s.

Below left: Six months after the end of steam on the Southern Region, Feltham shed stands deserted on 14 January 1968.

Right: Demolition is under way at a roofless Dalry Road shed on 4 September 1966.

Below: Withdrawn 'Black Fives' at Wigan Springs Branch on 11 May 1968. From right to left are Nos 45431, 45281, 45331 and 45226.

Bottom: No 45538 *Giggleswick*, one of five withdrawn unrebuilt 'Patriot' 4-6-0s at Rugby shed on 3 June 1962; the others were Nos 45537, 45541, 45542 and 45548.

Above: With pre-war double chimney and Peppercorn smoke deflectors, No 60097 *Humorist* was a funny A3 indeed! Leaving Forfar with the Glasgow-Aberdeen 'Bon Accord' on 12 September 1962, it passes Ivatt 2MT 2-6-0 No 46468 in the goods yard.

Below left: Stating the obvious? Barrow on 7 May 1966 . . .

Below: . . . and King's Cross on 5 June 1968.

102

So that's what the hole in the side-tank is for! Willesden shed, 30 January 1965.

"Look at that – only a penny and they could even put it on an enamel sign!" Bygone prices and stability recalled at Horsted Keynes on 13 July 1969.

Above: 'Large Prairie' No 6106 is in steam for an Open Day at the Didcot headquarters of the Great Western Society on 20 September 1969. Class 33 No 6500 runs past light engine.

Right: Pure Great Western at Buckfastleigh on 11 June 1967 – 0-4-2T No 1420, an auto-coach and a 'Toad' brake van.

Below: 'Coronation' No 46229 *Duchess of Hamilton* and 'Terrier' 0-6-0T No 32678 on 14 June 1967 at Butlin's Holiday Camp, Minehead, where they spent their early preservation years.

Right: The Keighley & Worth Valley Light Railway opened in June 1968. Visitors approach the booking hall at Haworth on 24 August 1969.

Below: There's time for a chat at Horsted Keynes on 13 July 1969 before P 0-6-0T No 27 (BR No 31027) departs with an afternoon Bluebell Railway train for Sheffield Park.

A3 No 4472 *Flying Scotsman* passes Woolmer Green on 17 May 1969 with a railtour from King's Cross to Diss, for Bressingham Gardens. A Class 31 with empty wagons has stopped by the signalbox while entering the double-track section through Welwyn and another, No D5648, has brought its ballast train close behind on the Up Goods line.

Above: No 4472 passes Wymondham on 15 September 1968, returning to its Doncaster base after working a railtour from Norwich to Chesterfield and back the previous day. The extra water-carrying tender was fitted to the A3 in late 1966.

Below: On 10 April 1965, *Flying Scotsman* arrives at Peterborough with a Pullman railtour organised by Alan Pegler for Darlington Works staff and their families, in appreciation of his A3's recent overhaul.

Above: Wolverhampton Low Level on 1 May 1965, with No 6849 *Walton Grange* (substituting for *Clun Castle*) on the Paddington-Minffordd Festiniog Railway AGM special.

Below: A4 No 60019 *Bittern* at Aberdeen at the head of the Scottish Region's 'A4 Farewell' railtour from Glasgow on 3 September 1966.

Above: 'Coronation' No 46245 *City of London* passes Knebworth with a Home Counties Railway Society King's Cross-Doncaster railtour on 9 June 1963.

Below: 'Battle of Britain' No 34089 *602 Squadron* approaches Barnes on 10 December 1966 with the LCGB 'Reunion Rail Tour'.

Above: 'Britannia' No 70052 *Firth of Tay* crosses the viaduct carrying the Midland main line over the River Lea and approaches Chiltern Green with the LCGB 'Notts & Lincs Railtour' from St.Pancras, 24 April 1965.

Above right: The Home Counties Railway Society King's Cross-York railtour of 4 October 1964 passes Knebworth behind No 70020 *Mercury*.

Right: Working from Manchester to Carlisle on the 'Fifteen Guinea Special', No 70013 *Oliver Cromwell* heads the final BR main-line steam train over Batty Moss Viaduct, Ribblehead, on 11 August 1968.

111

The view from Hanging Lund Scar as
Nos 44871 and 44781 approach Ais Gill on
the Carlisle-Liverpool return leg of the
'Fifteen Guinea Special', 11 August 1968.